Abide
in the Light

AN ADVENT PRAYER BOOK

PARK CITIES
PRESBYTERIAN CHURCH

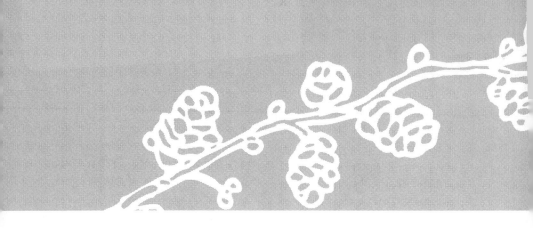

Arise, shine, for your light has come,
and the glory of the LORD has risen upon you.

Isaiah 60:1

Preface

∾

The Son of God, the second person in the Trinity, being very and eternal God, of one substance, and equal with the Father, did, when the fullness of time was come, take upon Him man's nature, with all the essential properties and common infirmities thereof; yet without sin: being conceived by the power of the Holy Ghost, in the womb of the virgin Mary, of her substance. So that two whole, perfect, and distinct natures, the Godhead and the manhood, were inseparably joined together in one person, without conversion, composition, or confusion. Which person is very God and very man, yet one Christ, the only mediator between God and man.

The Westminster Confession of Faith

Advent means arrival or coming. It is a time set apart to remember that God arrived in human history on earth in the person of Jesus Christ to save us from our sins. Jesus, the Light of the world, has come, and we rejoice at Advent as children of the Light.

Advent is also a time to rehearse the Christian hope for Jesus to come again, when the dwelling place of God shall be with His people, all things shall be well, and the Light that came to Bethlehem shall become the glorious incandescence of the new heavens and the new earth.

The daily Scripture readings walk through God's redemptive actions in history as revealed through key movements in the biblical story. Each Sunday of Advent is centered on prophecies and events that speak to Jesus's arrival and serve like trail markers along the path to Christmas.

May God use this Advent prayer book to draw you into the light of His presence, renewing you in the good news of great joy, Jesus our Savior.

INSTRUCTIONS ON USE

Advent begins on a different date each year and spans the four Sundays leading up to Christmas. 28 daily morning and evening prayers are given in this book to encompass the Advent season regardless of its duration in a particular year. Simply start with the daily prayers for the First Sunday in Advent and follow the prayers for each day until Christmas Eve. Prayers appointed for Christmas Eve can be found on page 146.

This prayer book can be used for a personal time of prayer or to assist prayer with others. The daily order guides prayer according to the Word of God and creates space for spontaneous prayers to emerge. When praying with others, one person should be appointed to read the words in light typeface while everyone else responds together with the words in bold typeface.

Call to Prayer

Hear God call you to abide with Him through His Word.

Scriptures are given to invite you into the presence of God in prayer.

Adoration

Delight in the goodness of God.

Scriptures are given that reflect awe and wonder in celebration of God.

Confession

Confess your sins to God.

A written prayer is given for the morning to offer biblically rooted words for confessing sin and to prompt personal and specific confession. Space is left open in the evening for self-examination and personal confession.

Thanksgiving

Give thanks to God.

Space is left open for personal expressions of gratitude to God.

Psalm

Pray with the people of God in the Psalms.

The Psalms are the prayer book of the people of God bringing the whole human experience before the face of God in faith. You may choose to read all the Psalms appointed for the day, one Psalm, or simply select a few verses.

Scripture Reading

Prayerfully read a portion of God's Word.

The daily Scripture readings walk through God's redemptive actions in history as revealed through key movements in the Biblical story. The Scripture readings appointed for each Sunday of Advent are centered on prophecies and events that speak to Jesus's arrival.

Silence

Keep a moment of quiet stillness to listen to God.

Space is offered to be silent before God, and a simple prayer is given for responding from a listening posture.

The Lord's Prayer

Pray the words that the Lord Jesus taught His disciples to pray.

The Lord's Prayer can be found on page 159.

Supplication

Earnestly ask God to accomplish His gracious will.

Written prayers are given morning and evening to express the desire for God's will to be done on earth as it is in Heaven. Personal prayers can be offered in addition to or in lieu of the given prayers.

Blessing

Receive God's transforming grace through His Word.

A Biblical blessing is given to encourage a life of prayer actively engaged in the world.

DAY 1

THE FIRST SUNDAY IN ADVENT

MORNING PRAYER

Call to Prayer

Hear God call you to abide with Him through His Word.

> Give ear to my words, O LORD;
>> consider my groaning.
>> **Give attention to the sound of my cry,**
>>> **my King and my God,**
>>> **for to you do I pray.**
>> O LORD, in the morning you hear my voice;
>>> in the morning I prepare a sacrifice for you and watch.   *Psalm 5:1-3*

Adoration

Delight in the goodness of God.

> O LORD, our Lord,
>> how majestic is your name in all the earth!
>> You have set your glory above the heavens.
>>> **Out of the mouth of babies and infants,**
>> **you have established strength because of your foes,**
>>> **to still the enemy and the avenger.**
>> When I look at your heavens, the work of your fingers,
>>> the moon and the stars, which you have set in place,

> *what is man that you are mindful of him,*
>> *and the son of man that you care for him?* Psalm 8:1-4

Confession

Confess your sins to God.

> **Have mercy on me, O God,**
>> **according to Your steadfast love;**
> **according to Your abundant mercy**
>> **blot out my transgressions.**
> **Wash me thoroughly from my iniquity,**
>> **and cleanse me from my sin! ...**
> **Restore to me the joy of your salvation,**
>> **and uphold me with a willing spirit. Amen.** Psalm 51:1-2, 12

Thanksgiving

Give thanks to God.

Psalm

Pray with the people of God in the Psalms.
Psalms 1-5

Scripture Reading

Prayerfully read a portion of God's Word.
Isaiah 60:1-3

Silence

Keep a moment of quiet stillness to listen to God.

> O God of peace, who hast taught us that in returning and rest we shall be
> saved, in quietness and in confidence shall be our strength: By the might

of Thy Spirit lift us, we pray Thee, to Thy presence, where we may be still and know that Thou art God, through Jesus Christ our Lord. ***Amen.***

To Be a Christian: An Anglican Catechism

The Lord's Prayer

Pray the words that the Lord Jesus taught His disciples to pray.

Supplication

Earnestly ask God to accomplish His gracious will.

Almighty God, give us grace that we may cast away the works of darkness, and put upon us the armor of light, now in the time of this mortal life, in which thy Son Jesus Christ came to visit us in great humility, that in the last day, when he shall come again in his glorious majesty, to judge both the quick and the dead, we may rise to the life immortal, through him who liveth and reigneth with thee and the Holy Ghost, now and forever. ***Amen.***   *The 1662 Book of Common Prayer*

Blessing

Receive God's transforming grace through His Word.

The grace of the Lord Jesus Christ and the love of God and the fellowship of the Holy Spirit be with you all.   *2 Corinthians 13:14*

EVENING PRAYER

Call to Prayer

Hear God call you to abide with Him through His Word.

For this reason I bow my knees before the Father, from whom every family in heaven and on earth is named, *that according to the riches of His glory He may grant you to be strengthened with power through His Spirit in your inner being, so that Christ may dwell in your hearts through faith*—that you, being rooted and grounded in love, may have strength to comprehend with all the saints what is the breadth and length and height and depth, *and to know the love of Christ that surpasses knowledge, that you may be filled with all the fullness of God.* *Ephesians 3:14-19*

Adoration

Delight in the goodness of God.

O LORD, God of Israel, there is no God like You, in heaven above or on earth beneath, keeping covenant and showing steadfast love to Your servants who walk before You with all their heart. 1 Kings 8:23

Confession

Confess your sins to God.

Thanksgiving

Give thanks to God.

Psalm

Pray with the people of God in the Psalms.

Psalms 6-8

Scripture Reading

Prayerfully read a portion of God's Word.

Isaiah 60:1-3

Silence

Keep a moment of quiet stillness to listen to God.

> Speak, LORD, for Your servant hears.   *1 Samuel 3:9*

The Lord's Prayer

Pray the words that the Lord Jesus taught His disciples to pray.

Supplication

Earnestly ask God to accomplish His gracious will.

> Answer me when I call, O God of my righteousness!
>> You have given me relief when I was in distress.
>> Be gracious to me and hear my prayer! . . .
> In peace I will both lie down and sleep;
>> for You alone, O LORD, make me dwell in safety. ***Amen.***   *Psalm 4:1, 8*

Blessing

Receive God's transforming grace through His Word.

> Blessed are your eyes, for they see, and your ears, for they hear.
> *Matthew 13:16*

DAY 2
MONDAY

MORNING PRAYER

Call to Prayer

Hear God call you to abide with Him through His Word.

> Make a joyful noise to the LORD, all the earth!
> > ***Serve the LORD with gladness!***
> > ***Come into His presence with singing!***
> Know that the LORD, he is God!
> > It is he who made us, and we are his;
> > we are his people, and the sheep of his pasture.   *Psalm 100:1-3*

Adoration

Delight in the goodness of God.

> Oh come, let us sing to the O LORD;
> > let us make a joyful noise to the rock of our salvation!
> ***Let us come into his presence with thanksgiving;***
> > ***let us make a joyful noise to Him with songs of praise!***
> For the LORD is a great God,
> > and a great King above all gods.
> ***In his hand are the depths of the earth;***
> > ***the heights of the mountains are his also.***

The sea is his, for he made it,
and his hands formed the dry land.   *Psalm 95:1-5*

Confession

Confess your sins to God.

O LORD, You have mercy upon all—take away from me my sins, and mercifully kindle in me the fire of your Holy Spirit. Take away from me the heart of stone, and give me a heart of flesh, a heart to love and adore You, a heart to delight in You, to follow and to enjoy You, for Christ's sake. Amen.   *Ambrose*

Thanksgiving

Give thanks to God.

Psalm

Pray with the people of God in the Psalms.
Psalms 9-11

Scripture Reading

Prayerfully read a portion of God's Word.
Genesis 1:1-2:3

Silence

Keep a moment of quiet stillness to listen to God.

Take our minds, and think through them. Take our lips, and speak through them. Take our hearts, and set them on fire with love for thee. What we know not, teach us. What we have not, give us. What we are not, make us. For Jesus Christ's sake. **Amen.**

The Lord's Prayer

Pray the words that the Lord Jesus taught His disciples to pray.

Supplication

Earnestly ask God to accomplish His gracious will.

Almighty God, our heavenly Father, who settest the solitary in families: Bless our homes, and put far from us, we beseech thee, all bitterness, the desire of vainglory, and the pride of life. Fill us with faith, virtue, knowledge, temperance, patience, and godliness. Knit together in constant affection those who, in holy wedlock, have been made one flesh; turn the heart of the fathers to the children, and the heart of the children to the fathers; and so enkindle fervent charity among us all, through Jesus Christ our Lord. ***Amen.***

Blessing

Receive God's transforming grace through His Word.

Jesus himself stood among them, and said to them, "Peace to you!"
Luke 24:36

EVENING PRAYER

Call to Prayer

Hear God call you to abide with Him through His Word.

But the hour is coming, and is now here, when the true worshipers will worship the Father in spirit and truth, *for the Father is seeking such people to worship him.*   John 4:23

Adoration

Delight in the goodness of God.

Blessed be the LORD who has given rest to his people Israel, according to all that he promised. Not one word has failed of all his good promise, which he spoke by Moses his servant. **The LORD our God be with us, as he was with our fathers. May he not leave us or forsake us,** *that he may incline our hearts to him, to walk in all his ways and to keep his commandments, his statutes, and his rules, which he commanded our fathers.*   1 Kings 8:56-58

Confession

Confess your sins to God.

Thanksgiving

Give thanks to God.

Psalm

Pray with the people of God in the Psalms.
Psalms 12-14

Scripture Reading

Prayerfully read a portion of God's Word.

Genesis 1:1-2:3

Silence

Keep a moment of quiet stillness to listen to God.

> For God alone my soul waits in silence;
>
> from him comes my salvation.
>
> He only is my rock and my salvation,
>
> my fortress; I shall not be greatly moved. ***Amen.*** *Psalm 62:1-2*

The Lord's Prayer

Pray the words that the Lord Jesus taught His disciples to pray.

Supplication

Earnestly ask God to accomplish His gracious will.

> Lighten our darkness, we beseech thee, O Lord; and by thy great mercy
> defend us from all perils and dangers of this night; for the love of thy only
> Son, our Savior, Jesus Christ. ***Amen.***
>
> *The 1662 Book of Common Prayer*

Blessing

Receive God's transforming grace through His Word.

> The Lord Jesus said, "Have you believed because you have seen me?
> Blessed are those who have not seen and yet have believed."
>
> *John 20:29*

DAY 3

TUESDAY

MORNING PRAYER

Call to Prayer

Hear God call you to abide with Him through His Word.

> Know that the LORD has set apart His faithful servant for Himself;
>> the LORD hears when I call to him.
> ***Tremble and do not sin;***
>> ***when you are on your beds,***
>> ***search your hearts and be silent.***
> Offer the sacrifices of the righteous
>> and trust in the LORD.   *Psalm 4:3-5*

Adoration

Delight in the goodness of God.

> How precious is Your steadfast love, O God!
>> The children of mankind take refuge in the shadow of your wings.
> ***They feast on the abundance of your house,***
>> ***and you give them drink from the river of your delights.***
> For with you is the fountain of life;
>> in your light do we see light.   Psalm 39:7-9

Confession

Confess your sins to God.

> *Cleanse me from my secret faults, O Lord, and forgive those offenses to your servant which he has caused in others. I contend not in judgment with You, who are truth; I fear to deceive myself, lest my sin should make me think that I am not sinful. Therefore, I content not in judgment with you; for if You, Lord, should mark iniquities, O Lord, who shall abide? Amen.*   *Augustine*

Thanksgiving

Give thanks to God.

Psalm

Pray with the people of God in the Psalms.
Psalms 15-17

Scripture Reading

Prayerfully read a portion of God's Word.
Psalm 8 and Genesis 2:4-25

Silence

Keep a moment of quiet stillness to listen to God.

Fix our hearts on thee, O God, in pure devotion, that the vain pursuits of this world may have no hold upon us, and that we may be changed, by the consuming fire of thy Spirit, into the image and likeness of thy Son, Jesus Christ our Lord, to whom, with thee and the same Spirit, be an honor and glory, world without end. ***Amen.***

The Lord's Prayer

Pray the words that the Lord Jesus taught His disciples to pray.

Supplication

Earnestly ask God to accomplish His gracious will.

Almighty God, our heavenly Father, who declares thy glory and showest forth thy handiwork in the heavens and in the earth: Deliver us, we beseech thee, in our several callings, from the service of Mammon, that we may do the work which thou givest us to do, in truth, in beauty, and in righteousness, with singleness of heart as thy servants, and to the benefit of our fellow men, for the sake of Him who came among us as one that serveth, thy Son, Jesus Christ our Lord. ***Amen.***

Blessing

Receive God's transforming grace through His Word.

The people who walked in darkness
have seen a great light;
those who dwelt in a land of deep darkness,
on them has light shone. *Isaiah 9:2*

EVENING PRAYER

Call to Prayer

Hear God call you to abide with Him through His Word.

> You are the light of the world. A city set on a hill cannot be hidden. ***Nor do people light a lamp and put it under a basket, but on a stand, and it gives light to all in the house.*** In the same way, let your light shine before others, so that they may see your good works and give glory to your Father who is in heaven.   *Matthew 5:14-16*

Adoration

Delight in the goodness of God.

> I bless the LORD who gives me counsel;
>   in the night also my heart instructs me.
> ***I have set the LORD always before me;***
>   ***because he is at my right hand, I shall not be shaken.***   *Psalm 16:7-8*

Confession

Confess your sins to God.

Thanksgiving

Give thanks to God.

Psalm

Pray with the people of God in the Psalms.
Psalm 18

Scripture Reading

Prayerfully read a portion of God's Word.

Psalm 8 and Genesis 2:4-25

Silence

Keep a moment of quiet stillness to listen to God.

> Behold, I am the servant of the Lord; let it be to me according to your
> word. ***Amen.***   *Luke 1:38*

The Lord's Prayer

Pray the words that the Lord Jesus taught His disciples to pray.

Supplication

Earnestly ask God to accomplish His gracious will.

> But you, O LORD, are a shield about me,
>   my glory, and the lifter of my head.
> I cried aloud to the LORD,
>   and he answered me from his holy hill. *Psalm 3:3-4*

Blessing

Receive God's transforming grace through His Word.

> May God be gracious to us and bless us
>   and make his face to shine upon us,
> that your way may be known on earth,
>   your saving power among all nations.
> Let the peoples praise you, O God;
>   let all the peoples praise you!   *Psalm 67:1-3*

DAY 4

WEDNESDAY

MORNING PRAYER

Call to Prayer

Hear God call you to abide with Him through His Word.

> I rise before dawn and cry for help;
>> I hope in your words.
>
> ***My eyes are awake before the watches of the night,***
>> ***that I may meditate on your promise.***
>
> Hear my voice according to your steadfast love;
>> O LORD, according to your justice give me life.   *Psalm 119:147-149*

Adoration

Delight in the goodness of God.

> Blessed are you, O LORD, the God of Israel our father, forever and ever.
> ***Yours, O LORD, is the greatness and the power and the glory and the***
> ***victory and the majesty, for all that is in the heavens and in the earth is***
> ***yours.*** Yours is the kingdom, O LORD, and you are exalted as head above
> all. ***Both riches and honor come from you, and you rule over all. In your***
> ***hand are power and might, and in your hand it is to make great and***
> ***to give strength to all.*** And now we thank you, our God, and praise your
> glorious name.   *1 Chronicles 29:10-13*

Confession

Confess your sins to God.

> **O Lord my God, light of the blind, and strength of the weak; yes, also light of those that see, and strength of the strong—hearken unto my soul, and hear it crying out of the depths. Woe is me! . . . Lord, help us to turn and seek You; for not as we have forsaken our Creator have You forsaken Your creation. Let us turn and seek You, for we know You are here in our heart, when we confess to You, when we cast ourselves upon You, and weep in Your bosom, after all our rugged ways; and You gently wipe away our tears, and we weep the more for joy; because You, Lord—not man of flesh and blood—but You, Lord, who made us, remake and comfort us. Amen.** *Augustine*

Thanksgiving

Give thanks to God.

Psalm

Pray with the people of God in the Psalms.

Psalms 19-21

Scripture Reading

Prayerfully read a portion of God's Word.

Genesis 3 and 4

Silence

Keep a moment of quiet stillness to listen to God.

O God of peace, who hast taught us that in returning and rest we shall be saved, in quietness and in confidence shall be our strength: By the might of thy Spirit lift us, we pray thee, to thy presence, where we may be still and know that thou art God, through Jesus Christ our Lord. **Amen.**

To Be a Christian: An Anglican Catechism

The Lord's Prayer

Pray the words that the Lord Jesus taught His disciples to pray.

Supplication

Earnestly ask God to accomplish His gracious will.

O God of unchangeable power and light eternal: Look favorably upon the body of thy whole church, and by thy eternal providence accomplish the salvation of man, that all the world may see and know that what was fallen has been lifted up, and what was grown old has been made new, and that all things are restored by Him through whom they were made, even thy Son Jesus Christ our Lord. **Amen.**

Blessing

Receive God's transforming grace through His Word.

The grace of the Lord Jesus Christ be with your spirit. *Philippians 4:23*

EVENING PRAYER

Call to Prayer

Hear God call you to abide with Him through His Word.

Therefore, as you received Christ Jesus the Lord, so walk in him, **rooted and built up in him and established in the faith, just as you were taught,** abounding in thanksgiving. *Colossians 2:6-7*

Adoration

Delight in the goodness of God.

How precious is your steadfast love, O God!
The children of mankind take refuge in the shadow of your wings.
They feast on the abundance of your house,
and you give them drink from the river of your delights.
For with you is the fountain of life;
in your light do we see light. *Psalm 36:7-9*

Confession

Confess your sins to God.

Thanksgiving

Give thanks to God.

Psalm

Pray with the people of God in the Psalms.
Psalms 22-23

Scripture Reading

Prayerfully read a portion of God's Word.

Genesis 3 and 4

Silence

Keep a moment of quiet stillness to listen to God.

Speak, LORD, for your servant hears. ***Amen.*** *1 Samuel 3:9*

The Lord's Prayer

Pray the words that the Lord Jesus taught His disciples to pray.

Supplication

Earnestly ask God to accomplish His gracious will.

As a reconciled Father, take me to be your child; and give me your renewing Spirit, to be in me a principle of holy life, and light, and love, and your seal and witness that I am yours. Let him quicken my dead and hardened heart. Let him enlighten my dark and unbelieving mind, by clearer knowledge and firm belief. Let him turn my will to the ready obedience of your holy will. Let him reveal to my soul the wonders of your love in Christ, and fill it with love to you and my Redeemer, and to all your holy Word and works. ***Amen.*** *Richard Baxter*

Blessing

Receive God's transforming grace through His Word.

But we do not want you to be uninformed, brothers, about those who are asleep, that you may not grieve as others do who have no hope. For since we believe that Jesus died and rose again, even so, through Jesus, God will bring with him those who have fallen asleep. *1 Thessalonians 4:13-14*

DAY 5
THURSDAY

MORNING PRAYER

Call to Prayer

Hear God call you to abide with Him through His Word.

> Sing praises to the LORD, O you his saints,
>> and give thanks to his holy name.
>> ***For his anger is but for a moment,***
>> ***and his favor is for a lifetime.***
>> Weeping may tarry for the night,
>> but joy comes with the morning.   *Psalm 30:4-5*

Adoration

Delight in the goodness of God.

> Your steadfast love, O LORD, extends to the heavens,
>> your faithfulness to the clouds.
>> ***Your righteousness is like the mountains of God;***
>> ***your judgments are like the great deep;***
>> ***man and beast you save, O LORD.***   *Psalm 36:5-6*

Confession

Confess your sins to God.

> *O You plenteous source of every good and perfect gift, shed abroad the cheering light of Your sevenfold grace over our hearts. Yes, Spirit of love and gentleness, we most humbly implore Your assistance. You know our faults, our failings, our necessities, the dullness of our understanding, the waywardness of our affections, the perverseness of our will. When, therefore, we neglect to practice what we know, visit us, we ask You, with Your grace; enlighten our minds, rectify our desires, correct our wanderings, and pardon our omissions, so that by Your guidance we may be preserved from making shipwreck of faith, and keep a good conscience, and may at length be landed safe in the haven of eternal rest; through Jesus Christ our Lord. Amen.*   Anselm

Thanksgiving

Give thanks to God.

Psalm

Pray with the people of God in the Psalms.
Psalms 24-26

Scripture Reading

Prayerfully read a portion of God's Word.
Genesis 6 and 9

Silence

Keep a moment of quiet stillness to listen to God.

> Take our minds, and think through them. Take our lips, and speak through them. Take our hearts, and set them on fire with love for thee.

What we know not, teach us. What we have not, give us. What we are not, make us. For Jesus Christ's sake. ***Amen.***

The Lord's Prayer

Pray the words that the Lord Jesus taught His disciples to pray.

Supplication

Earnestly ask God to accomplish His gracious will.

Almighty God, who by thy Son Jesus Christ didst give commandment to the apostles, that they should go into all the world and preach the gospel to every creature: Grant to us, whom thou hast called into they church, a ready will to obey thy word, and fill us with a hearty desire to make thy way known upon earth, thy saving health among all nations. Look with compassion upon the peoples that have not known thee, and upon the multitudes that are scattered abroad as sheep having no shepherd, and gather them into thy fold, through the same Jesus Christ our Lord. ***Amen.***

Blessing

Receive God's transforming grace through His Word.

The Lord Jesus said: "Peace be with you! As the Father has sent me, I am sending you."   *John 20:21*

EVENING PRAYER

Call to Prayer

Hear God call you to abide with Him through His Word.

> So faith comes from hearing, **and hearing through the word of Christ.**
> *Romans 10:17*

Adoration

Delight in the goodness of God.

> I will extol you, my God and King,
>   and bless your name forever and ever.
> **Every day I will bless you**
>   **and praise your name forever and ever.**
> Great is the LORD, and greatly to be praised,
>   and his greatness is unsearchable.   *Psalm 145:1-3*

Confession

Confess your sins to God.

Thanksgiving

Give thanks to God.

Psalm

Pray with the people of God in the Psalms.
Psalms 27-29

Scripture Reading

Prayerfully read a portion of God's Word.
Genesis 6 and 9

Silence

Keep a moment of quiet stillness to listen to God.

> For God alone my soul waits in silence;
> from him comes my salvation.
> He only is my rock and my salvation,
> my fortress; I shall not be greatly moved. ***Amen****. Psalm 62:1-2*

The Lord's Prayer

Pray the words that the Lord Jesus taught His disciples to pray.

Supplication

Earnestly ask God to accomplish His gracious will.

> Keep watch, dear Lord, with those who work, or watch, or weep this night, and give thine angels charge over those who sleep. Tend the sick, Lord Christ, give rest to the weary, bless the dying, soothe the suffering, pity the afflicted, shield the joyous, and all for thy love's sake. ***Amen***.

Blessing

Receive God's transforming grace through His Word.

> For I want you to know how great a struggle I have for you and for those at Laodicea and for all who have not seen me face to face, that their hearts may be encouraged, being knit together in love, to reach all the riches of full assurance of understanding and the knowledge of God's mystery, which is Christ, in whom are hidden all the treasures of wisdom and knowledge. *Colossians 2:1-3*

DAY 6
FRIDAY

MORNING PRAYER

Call to Prayer

Hear God call you to abide with Him through His Word.

> One thing have I asked of the LORD,
>   that will I seek after:
> ***that I may dwell in the house of the LORD***
>   ***all the days of my life,***
> to gaze upon the beauty of the LORD
>   and to inquire in his temple.   *Psalm 27:4*

Adoration

Delight in the goodness of God.

> The heavens declare the glory of God,
>   and the sky above proclaims his handiwork.
> ***Day to day pours out speech,***
>   ***and night to night reveals knowledge.***
> There is no speech, nor are there words,
>   whose voice is not heard.   *Psalm 19:1-3*

Confession

Confess your sins to God.

> Lord Jesus Christ, great was Your goodness in undertaking my redemption, in consenting to be made sin for me, in conquering all my foes. Great was Your love in manifesting Yourself alive, in showing Your sacred wounds, that every fear might vanish, and every doubt be removed. Great was Your mercy in ascending to heaven, in being crowned and enthroned there to intercede for me, there to help me in temptation, there to open the eternal book, there to receive me finally to Yourself. Great was Your wisdom in devising this means of salvation; bathe my soul in rich consolations of Your resurrection life. O God, pardon all my sins, known and unknown, felt and unfelt, confessed and not confessed, remembered or forgotten. Grant me more and more of the resurrection life: may it rule me, may I walk in its power, and be strengthened through its influence. Amen.

The Valley of Vision: A Collection of Puritan Prayers & Devotions

Thanksgiving

Give thanks to God.

Psalm

Pray with the people of God in the Psalms.

Psalms 30-31

Scripture Reading

Prayerfully read a portion of God's Word.

Genesis 12; 18:1-15; 22

Silence

Keep a moment of quiet stillness to listen to God.

Fix our hearts on thee, O God, in pure devotion, that the vain pursuits of this world may have no hold upon us, and that we may be changed, by the consuming fire of thy Spirit, into the image and likeness of thy Son, Jesus Christ our Lord, to whom, with thee and the same Spirit, be an honor and glory, world without end. ***Amen.***

The Lord's Prayer

Pray the words that the Lord Jesus taught His disciples to pray.

Supplication

Earnestly ask God to accomplish His gracious will.

O Lord, have mercy upon us. O Christ, have mercy upon us. O Spirit, have mercy upon us. ***Amen.***   *Gregory the Great*

Blessing

Receive God's transforming grace through His Word.

The God of peace will soon crush Satan under your feet. The grace of our Lord Jesus Christ be with you.   *Romans 16:20*

EVENING PRAYER

Call to Prayer

Hear God call you to abide with Him through His Word.

Grace to you and peace from God our Father and the Lord Jesus Christ, ***who gave himself for our sins to deliver us from the present evil age,*** according to the will of our God and Father, ***to whom be the glory forever and ever.*** *Galatians 1:3-5*

Adoration

Delight in the goodness of God.

Who is this King of glory?
The LORD of hosts,
he is the King of glory! *Psalm 24:10*

Confession

Confess your sins to God.

Thanksgiving

Give thanks to God.

Psalm

Pray with the people of God in the Psalms.
Psalms 32-34

Scripture Reading

Prayerfully read a portion of God's Word.
Genesis 12; 18:1-15; 22

Silence

Keep a moment of quiet stillness to listen to God.

Behold, I am the servant of the Lord; let it be to me according to your word. **Amen.** *Luke 1:38*

The Lord's Prayer

Pray the words that the Lord Jesus taught His disciples to pray.

Supplication

Earnestly ask God to accomplish His gracious will.

O Merciful Lord God, heavenly Father, whether we sleep or wake, live or die, we are always thine. Wherefore I beseech thee heartily to take care and charge of me, not suffering me to perish in the works of darkness, but kindling the light of thy countenance in my heart, that thy godly knowledge may daily increase in me, through a right and pure faith, and that I may always be found to walk and live after thy wisdom and pleasure, through Jesus Christ our Lord and Savior. **Amen.**

Blessing

Receive God's transforming grace through His Word.

It is in vain that you rise up early
   and go late to rest,
eating the bread of anxious toil;
   for he gives to his beloved sleep. *Psalm 127:2*

DAY 7
SATURDAY

MORNING PRAYER

Call to Prayer

Hear God call you to abide with Him through His Word.

> I believe that I shall look upon the goodness of the LORD
> in the land of the living!
> **Wait for the LORD;**
> **be strong, and let your heart take courage;**
> **wait for the LORD!** *Psalm 27:13-14*

Adoration

Delight in the goodness of God.

> A Psalm of David.
> The LORD is my shepherd; I shall not want.
> **He makes me lie down in green pastures.**
> **He leads me beside still waters.**
> He restores my soul.
> He leads me in paths of righteousness
> for his name's sake.
> **Even though I walk through the valley of the shadow of death,**
> **I will fear no evil,**

for you are with me;
  your rod and your staff,
  they comfort me.
You prepare a table before me
  in the presence of my enemies;
you anoint my head with oil;
  my cup overflows.
Surely goodness and mercy shall follow me
  all the days of my life,
and I shall dwell in the house of the Lord
  forever.   Psalm 23

Confession

Confess your sins to God.

Almighty and everlasting God, You hate nothing You have made, and You forgive the sins of all who are penitent: Create and make in us new and contrite hearts, that we, worthily lamenting our sins and acknowledging wretchedness, may obtain of You, the God of all mercy, perfect remission and forgiveness; through Jesus Christ our Lord; who lives and reigns with You and the Holy Spirit, one God, for ever and ever. Amen.   To Be a Christian: An Anglican Catechism

Thanksgiving

Give thanks to God.

Psalm

Pray with the people of God in the Psalms.
Psalms 35-36

Scripture Reading

Prayerfully read a portion of God's Word.

Genesis 28:10-22 and 45:1-28

Silence

Keep a moment of quiet stillness to listen to God.

> O God of peace, who hast taught us that in returning and rest we shall be saved, in quietness and in confidence shall be our strength: By the might of thy Spirit lift us, we pray thee, to thy presence, where we may be still and know that thou art God, through Jesus Christ our Lord. *Amen.*
> *To Be a Christian: An Anglican Catechism*

The Lord's Prayer

Pray the words that the Lord Jesus taught His disciples to pray.

Supplication

Earnestly ask God to accomplish His gracious will.

> O Lord, who hast brought us through the darkness of night to the light of morning, and who by thy Holy Spirit dost illumine the darkness of ignorance and sin: We beseech thee of thy loving-kindness to pour thy holy light into our souls, that we may be ever devoted to thee, by whose wisdom we were created, by whose mercy we were redeemed, and by whose providence we are governed, to the honor and glory of thy great name. *Amen.*

Blessing

Receive God's transforming grace through His Word.

> Peace be to the brothers, and love with faith, from God the Father and the Lord Jesus Christ. Grace be with all who love our Lord Jesus Christ with love incorruptible. *Ephesians 6:23-24*

EVENING PRAYER

Call to Prayer

Hear God call you to abide with Him through His Word.

Blessed be the God and Father of our Lord Jesus Christ, who has blessed us in Christ with every spiritual blessing in the heavenly places, ***even as he chose us in him before the foundation of the world, that we should be holy and blameless before him.*** *Ephesians 1:3-4*

Adoration

Delight in the goodness of God.

All the ends of the earth shall remember
   and turn to the LORD,
and all the families of the nations
   shall worship before you.
For kingship belongs to the LORD,
   and he rules over the nations. *Psalm 22:27-28*

Confession

Confess your sins to God.

Thanksgiving

Give thanks to God.

Psalm

Pray with the people of God in the Psalms.
Psalm 37

Scripture Reading

Prayerfully read a portion of God's Word.

Genesis 28:10-22 and 45:1-28

Silence

Keep a moment of quiet stillness to listen to God.

> *Speak, LORD, for your servant hears.* **Amen.** *1 Samuel 3:9*

The Lord's Prayer

Pray the words that the Lord Jesus taught His disciples to pray.

Supplication

Earnestly ask God to accomplish His gracious will.

> O God, from whom all holy desires, all good counsels, and all just works do proceed: Give unto thy servants that peace which the world cannot give; that both our hearts may be set to obey thy commandments, and also that by thee we being defended from the fear of our enemies may pass our time in rest and quietness; through the merits of Jesus Christ our Savior. **Amen.** *The 1662 Book of Common Prayer*

Blessing

Receive God's transforming grace through His Word.

> May the Lord direct your hearts to the love of God and to the stead-fastness of Christ. *2 Thessalonians 3:5*

DAY 8
THE SECOND SUNDAY IN ADVENT

MORNING PRAYER

Call to Prayer

Hear God call you to abide with Him through His Word.

> Open my eyes, **that I may behold**
> **wondrous things out of your law.**   *Psalm 119:18*

Adoration

Delight in the goodness of God.

> *God is our refuge and strength,*
> **a very present help in trouble.**   *Psalm 46:1*

Confession

Confess your sins to God.

> **Have mercy on me, O God,**
> **according to Your steadfast love;**
> **according to Your abundant mercy**
> **blot out my transgressions.**
> **Wash me thoroughly from my iniquity,**
> **and cleanse me from my sin! . . .**
> **Restore to me the joy of your salvation,**
> **and uphold me with a willing spirit. Amen.** *Psalm 51:1-2, 12*

Thanksgiving

Give thanks to God.

Psalm

Pray with the people of God in the Psalms.
Psalms 38-40

Scripture Reading

Prayerfully read a portion of God's Word.
Isaiah 9:2-7 and Isaiah 11:1-9

Silence

Keep a moment of quiet stillness to listen to God.

Take our minds, and think through them. Take our lips, and speak through them. Take our hearts, and set them on fire with love for thee. What we know not, teach us. What we have not, give us. What we are not, make us. For Jesus Christ's sake. ***Amen.***

The Lord's Prayer

Pray the words that the Lord Jesus taught His disciples to pray.

Supplication

Earnestly ask God to accomplish His gracious will.

Almighty God, give us grace that we may cast away the works of darkness, and put upon us the armor of light, now in the time of this mortal life, in which thy Son Jesus Christ came to visit us in great humility, that in the last day, when he shall come again in his glorious majesty, to judge both the quick and the dead, we may rise to the life immortal, through him who liveth and reigneth with thee and the Holy Ghost, now and forever. ***Amen.***

The 1662 Book of Common Prayer

Blessing

Receive God's transforming grace through His Word.

> In him we have redemption through his blood, the forgiveness of our trespasses, according to the riches of his grace, which he lavished upon us, in all wisdom and insight making known to us the mystery of his will, according to his purpose, which he set forth in Christ as a plan for the fullness of time, to unite all things in him, things in heaven and things on earth. *Ephesians 1:7-10*

EVENING PRAYER

Call to Prayer

Hear God call you to abide with Him through His Word.

Therefore, confess your sins to one another and pray for one another, that you may be healed. ***The prayer of a righteous person has great power as it is working.*** *James 5:16*

Adoration

Delight in the goodness of God.

Oh, the depth of the riches and wisdom and knowledge of God! How unsearchable are his judgments and how inscrutable his ways!!

"For who has known the mind of the Lord,
or who has been his counselor?"

"Or who has given a gift to him
that he might be repaid?"

For from him and through him and to him are all things. To him be glory forever. Amen. *Romans 11:33-36*

Confession

Confess your sins to God.

Thanksgiving

Give thanks to God.

Psalm

Pray with the people of God in the Psalms.

Psalms 41-43

Scripture Reading

Prayerfully read a portion of God's Word.

Isaiah 9:2-7 and Isaiah 11:1-9

Silence

Keep a moment of quiet stillness to listen to God.

> For God alone my soul waits in silence;
>> from him comes my salvation.
> He only is my rock and my salvation,
>> my fortress; I shall not be greatly moved. ***Amen.*** *Psalm 62:1-2*

The Lord's Prayer

Pray the words that the Lord Jesus taught His disciples to pray.

Supplication

Earnestly ask God to accomplish His gracious will.

> Answer me when I call, O God of my righteousness!
>> You have given me relief when I was in distress.
>> Be gracious to me and hear my prayer! . . .
> In peace I will both lie down and sleep;
>> for you alone, O LORD, make me dwell in safety. ***Amen.*** *Psalm 4:1, 8*

Blessing

Receive God's transforming grace through His Word.

> But God, being rich in mercy, because of the great love with which he loved us, even when we were dead in our trespasses, made us alive together with Christ—by grace you have been saved. *Ephesians 2:4-6*

DAY 9

MORNING PRAYER

Call to Prayer

Hear God call you to abide with Him through His Word.

> Satisfy us in the morning with your steadfast love,
>> that we may rejoice and be glad all our days.
>
> ***Make us glad for as many days as you have afflicted us,***
>> ***and for as many years as we have seen evil.***
>
> Let your work be shown to your servants,
>> and your glorious power to their children.
>
> ***Let the favor of the LORD our God be upon us,***
>> ***and establish the work of our hands upon us;***
>>> ***yes, establish the work of our hands!*** *Psalm 90:14-17*

Adoration

Delight in the goodness of God.

> Oh sing to the LORD a new song;
>> sing to the LORD, all the earth!
>
> ***Sing to the LORD, bless his name;***
>> ***tell of his salvation from day to day.***
>
> Declare his glory among the nations,

his marvelous works among all the peoples!

For great is the LORD, and greatly to be praised;
   he is to be feared above all gods.
For all the gods of the peoples are worthless idols,
   but the LORD made the heavens.
Splendor and majesty are before him;
   strength and beauty are in his sanctuary.   *Psalm 96:1-6*

Confession

Confess your sins to God.

O Lord, You have mercy upon all—take away from me my sins, and mercifully kindle in me the fire of Your Holy Spirit. Take away from me the heart of stone, and give me a heart of flesh, a heart to love and adore You, a heart to delight in You, to follow and to enjoy You, for Christ's sake. Amen.   *Ambrose*

Thanksgiving

Give thanks to God.

Psalm

Pray with the people of God in the Psalms.
Psalms 44-46

Scripture Reading

Prayerfully read a portion of God's Word.
Exodus 3 and 15:1-21

Silence

Keep a moment of quiet stillness to listen to God.

Fix our hearts on thee, O God, in pure devotion, that the vain pursuits of this world may have no hold upon us, and that we may be changed, by the consuming fire of thy Spirit, into the image and likeness of thy Son, Jesus Christ our Lord, to whom, with thee and the same Spirit, be an honor and glory, world without end. ***Amen.***

The Lord's Prayer

Pray the words that the Lord Jesus taught His disciples to pray.

Supplication

Earnestly ask God to accomplish His gracious will.

Almighty and eternal God, so draw our hearts to you, so guide our minds, so fill our imaginations, so control our wills, that we may be wholly yours, utterly dedicated to you; and then use us, we pray, as you will, and always to your glory and the welfare of your people; through our Lord and Savior Jesus Christ. ***Amen.*** *To Be a Christian: An Anglican Catechism*

Blessing

Receive God's transforming grace through His Word.

Now may the Lord of peace himself give you peace at all times in every way. The Lord be with you all. *2 Thessalonians 3:16*

EVENING PRAYER

Call to Prayer

Hear God call you to abide with Him through His Word.

> I appeal to you therefore, brothers by the mercies of God, **to present your bodies as a living sacrifice, holy and acceptable to God,** which is your spiritual worship.   *Romans 12:1*

Adoration

Delight in the goodness of God.

> Ascribe to the LORD, O families of the peoples,
>   ascribe to the LORD glory and strength!
> **Ascribe to the LORD the glory due his name;**
>   **bring an offering, and come into his courts!**
> Worship the LORD in the splendor of holiness;
>   tremble before him, all the earth!   *Psalm 96:7-9*

Confession

Confess your sins to God.

Thanksgiving

Give thanks to God.

Psalm

Pray with the people of God in the Psalms.
Psalms 47-49

Scripture Reading

Prayerfully read a portion of God's Word.

Exodus 3 and 15:1-21

Silence

Keep a moment of quiet stillness to listen to God.

> Behold, I am the servant of the Lord; let it be to me according to your
> word. ***Amen.*** *Luke 1:38*

The Lord's Prayer

Pray the words that the Lord Jesus taught His disciples to pray.

Supplication

Earnestly ask God to accomplish His gracious will.

> Lighten our darkness, we beseech thee, O Lord; and by thy great mercy
> defend us from all perils and dangers of this night; for the love of thy only
> Son, our Savior, Jesus Christ. ***Amen.***
> *The 1662 Book of Common Prayer*

Blessing

Receive God's transforming grace through His Word.

> "Death is swallowed up in victory."
> "O death, where is your victory?
> O death, where is your sting?"
> The sting of death is sin, and the power of sin is the law. But thanks
> be to God, who gives us the victory through our Lord Jesus Christ.
> *1 Corinthians 15:55-57*

DAY 10

TUESDAY

MORNING PRAYER

Call to Prayer

Hear God call you to abide with Him through His Word.

> Behold, the Lord GOD comes with might,
>   and his arm rules for him;
> **behold, his reward is with him,**
>   **and his recompense before him.**
> He will tend his flock like a shepherd;
>   he will gather the lambs in his arms;
> **he will carry them in his bosom,**
>   **and gently lead those that are with young.**   *Isaiah 40:10-11*

Adoration

Delight in the goodness of God.

> Oh sing to the LORD a new song,
>   for he has done marvelous things!
> **His right hand and his holy arm**
>   **have worked salvation for him.**
> The LORD has made known his salvation;
>   he has revealed his righteousness in the sight of the nations.

He has remembered his steadfast love and faithfulness
to the house of Israel.

All the ends of the earth have seen
the salvation of our God.   *Psalm 98:1-3*

Confession

Confess your sins to God.

> *Cleanse me from my secret faults, O Lord, and forgive those offenses to Your servant which he has caused in others. I contend not in judgment with You, who are truth; I fear to deceive myself, lest my sin should make me think that I am not sinful. Therefore, I contend not in judgment with You; for if You, Lord, should mark iniquities, O Lord, who shall abide? Amen.* Augustine

Thanksgiving

Give thanks to God.

Psalm

Pray with the people of God in the Psalms.
Psalms 50-52

Scripture Reading

Prayerfully read a portion of God's Word.
Exodus 19 and 20

Silence

Keep a moment of quiet stillness to listen to God.

O God of peace, who hast taught us that in returning and rest we shall be saved, in quietness and in confidence shall be our strength: By the might of thy Spirit lift us, we pray thee, to thy presence, where we may be

still and know that thou art God, through Jesus Christ our Lord. . ***Amen.***
To Be a Christian: An Anglican Catechism

The Lord's Prayer

Pray the words that the Lord Jesus taught His disciples to pray.

Supplication

Earnestly ask God to accomplish His gracious will.

Merciful God, who hast given unto us all things that pertain unto life and godliness: Grant that we may be faithful in the exercise of our duties; and that whatsoever thou givest us to do, we may do it heartily, as unto thee, O Lord, and not unto men, through Him who hast called us to glory and virtue, Jesus Christ, thy Son, our Lord. ***Amen.***

Blessing

Receive God's transforming grace through His Word.

The Lord be with your spirit. Grace be with you.   *2 Timothy 4:22*

EVENING PRAYER

Call to Prayer

Hear God call you to abide with Him through His Word.

Ask, and it will be given to you; seek, and you will find; knock, and it will be opened to you. ***For everyone who asks receives, and the one who seeks finds, and to the one who knocks it will be opened.*** Or which one of you, if his son asks him for bread, will give him a stone? Or if he asks for a fish, will give him a serpent? ***If you then, who are evil, know how to give good gifts to your children, how much more will your Father who is in heaven give good things to those who ask him!*** *Matthew 7:7-11*

Adoration

Delight in the goodness of God.

I give you thanks, O LORD, with my whole heart;
  before the gods I sing your praise;
I bow down toward your holy temple
    and give thanks to your name for your steadfast love and your
faithfulness,
  for you have exalted above all things
  your name and your word.
On the day I called, you answered me;
  my strength of soul you increased. *Psalm 138:1-3*

Confession

Confess your sins to God.

Thanksgiving

Give thanks to God.

Psalm

Pray with the people of God in the Psalms.

Psalms 53-55

Scripture Reading

Prayerfully read a portion of God's Word.

Exodus 19 and 20

Silence

Keep a moment of quiet stillness to listen to God.

> Speak, LORD, for your servant hears. **Amen**. *1 Samuel 3:9*

The Lord's Prayer

Pray the words that the Lord Jesus taught His disciples to pray.

Supplication

Earnestly ask God to accomplish His gracious will.

> But you, O LORD, are a shield about me,
>   my glory, and the lifter of my head.
> I cried aloud to the LORD,
>   and he answered me from his holy hill. *Psalm 3:3-4*

Blessing

Receive God's transforming grace through His Word.

> Now may the God of peace who brought again from the dead our Lord Jesus, the great shepherd of the sheep, by the blood of the eternal covenant, equip you with everything good that you may do his will, working in us that which is pleasing in his sight, through Jesus Christ, to whom be glory forever and ever. ***Amen.*** *Hebrews 13:20-21*

DAY 11
WEDNESDAY

MORNING PRAYER

Call to Prayer

Hear God call you to abide with Him through His Word.

> I call upon you, for you will answer me, O God;
> incline your ear to me; hear my words.
> **Wondrously show your steadfast love,**
> **O Savior of those who seek refuge**
> **from their adversaries at your right hand.**
> Keep me as the apple of your eye;
> hide me in the shadow of your wings.   *Psalm 17:6-8*

Adoration

Delight in the goodness of God.

> Let them thank the LORD for his steadfast love,
> for his wondrous works to the children of man!
> **For he satisfies the longing soul,**
> **and the hungry soul he fills with good things.**   *Psalm 107:8-9*

Confession

Confess your sins to God.

> **O Lord my God, light of the blind, and strength of the weak; yes, also light of those that see, and strength of the strong—hearken unto my soul, and hear it crying out of the depths. Woe is me! . . . Lord, help us to turn and seek You; for not as we have forsaken our Creator have You forsaken Your creation. Let us turn and seek You, for we know You are here in our heart, when we confess to You, when we cast ourselves upon You, and weep in Your bosom, after all our rugged ways; and You gently wipe away our tears, and we weep the more for joy; because You, Lord—not man of flesh and blood—but You, Lord, who made us, remake and comfort us. Amen.** *Augustine*

Thanksgiving

Give thanks to God.

Psalm

Pray with the people of God in the Psalms.
Psalms 56-58

Scripture Reading

Prayerfully read a portion of God's Word.
Exodus 40

Silence

Keep a moment of quiet stillness to listen to God.

Take our minds, and think through them. Take our lips, speak through them. Take our hearts, and set them on fire with love for thee. What we know not, teach us. What we have not, give us. What we are not, make us. For Jesus Christ's sake. ***Amen.***

The Lord's Prayer

Pray the words that the Lord Jesus taught His disciples to pray.

Supplication

Earnestly ask God to accomplish His gracious will.

O God our Savior, who willest that all men should be saved and come to the knowledge of the truth: Prosper, we pray thee, those who labor in distant lands. Protect them in all perils, and supply their every need. Give them grace to bear faithful witness unto thee, and endue them with burning zeal and love, that they may turn many to righteousness, and finally obtain a crown of glory, through Jesus Christ our Lord. ***Amen.***

Blessing

Receive God's transforming grace through His Word.

Blessed be the God and Father of our Lord Jesus Christ! According to his great mercy, he has caused us to be born again to a living hope through the resurrection of Jesus Christ from the dead, to an inheritance that is imperishable, undefiled, and unfading, kept in heaven for you, who by God's power are being guarded through faith for a salvation ready to be revealed in the last time.   *1 Peter 1:3-5*

EVENING PRAYER

Call to Prayer

Hear God call you to abide with Him through His Word.

Then Jesus told His disciples, "If anyone would come after me, *let him deny himself and take up his cross and follow me."* *Matthew 16:24*

Adoration

Delight in the goodness of God.

All the kings of the earth shall give you thanks, O LORD,
for they have heard the words of your mouth,
and they shall sing of the ways of the LORD,
for great is the glory of the LORD.
For though the LORD is high, he regards the lowly,
but the haughty he knows from afar.   *Psalm 138:4-6*

Confession

Confess your sins to God.

Thanksgiving

Give thanks to God.

Psalm

Pray with the people of God in the Psalms.
Psalms 59-61

Scripture Reading

Prayerfully read a portion of God's Word.
Exodus 40

Silence

Keep a moment of quiet stillness to listen to God.

> For God alone my soul waits in silence;
>> from him comes my salvation.
> He only is my rock and my salvation,
>> my fortress; I shall not be greatly moved. ***Amen.*** *Psalm 62:1-2*

The Lord's Prayer

Pray the words that the Lord Jesus taught His disciples to pray.

Supplication

Earnestly ask God to accomplish His gracious will.

As a reconciled Father, take me to be your child; and give me your renewing Spirit, to be in me a principle of holy life, and light, and love, and your seal and witness that I am yours. Let him quicken my dead and hardened heart. Let him enlighten my dark and unbelieving mind, by clearer knowledge and firm belief. Let him turn my will to the ready obedience of your holy will. Let him reveal to my soul the wonders of your love in Christ, and fill it with love to you and my Redeemer, and to all your holy Word and works. ***Amen.*** *Richard Baxter*

Blessing

Receive God's transforming grace through His Word.

> He who testifies to these things says, "Surely I am coming soon." ***Amen.***
> Come, Lord Jesus!
> The grace of the Lord Jesus be with all. ***Amen.*** *Revelation 22:20-21*

DAY 12

THURSDAY

MORNING PRAYER

Call to Prayer

Hear God call you to abide with Him through His Word.

> Fear not, for I am with you;
>> be not dismayed, for I am your God;
> **I will strengthen you, I will help you,**
>> **I will uphold you with my righteous right hand.**   *Isaiah 41:9-10*

Adoration

Delight in the goodness of God.

> All your works shall give thanks to you, O LORD,
>> and all your saints shall bless you!
> **They shall speak of the glory of your kingdom**
>> **and tell of your power,**
> to make known to the children of man your mighty deeds,
>> and the glorious splendor of your kingdom.
> **Your kingdom is an everlasting kingdom,**
>> **and your dominion endures throughout all generations.**
> *Psalm 145:10-13*

Confession

Confess your sins to God.

> **O You plenteous source of every good and perfect gift, shed abroad the cheering light of Your sevenfold grace over our hearts. Yes, Spirit of love and gentleness, we most humbly implore Your assistance. You know our faults, our failings, our necessities, the dullness of our understanding, the waywardness of our affections, the perverseness of our will. When, therefore, we neglect to practice what we know, visit us, we ask You, with Your grace; enlighten our minds, rectify our desires, correct our wanderings, and pardon our omissions, so that by Your guidance we may be preserved from making shipwreck of faith, and keep a good conscience, and may at length be landed safe in the haven of eternal rest; through Jesus Christ our Lord. Amen.** *Anselm*

Thanksgiving

Give thanks to God.

Psalm

Pray with the people of God in the Psalms.
Psalms 62-64

Scripture Reading

Prayerfully read a portion of God's Word.
Joshua 1 and 24:1-28

Silence

Keep a moment of quiet stillness to listen to God.

Fix our hearts on thee, O God, in pure devotion, that the vain pursuits of this world may have no hold upon us, and that we may be changed, by the consuming fire of thy Spirit, into the image and likeness of thy Son, Jesus

Christ our Lord, to whom, with thee and the same Spirit, be an honor and glory, world without end. *Amen.*

The Lord's Prayer

Pray the words that the Lord Jesus taught His disciples to pray.

Supplication

Earnestly ask God to accomplish His gracious will.

O Lord, our heavenly Father, whose blessed Son came not to be ministered unto, but to minister: We beseech thee to bless all who, following in His steps, give themselves to the service of their fellow men. Endue them with wisdom, patience, and courage, to strengthen the weak and raise up those who fall, that, being inspired by thy love, they may worthily minister in thy name to the suffering, the friendless, and the needy, for the sake of Him who laid down His life for us, the same thy Son our Savior Jesus Christ. *Amen.*

Blessing

Receive God's transforming grace through His Word.

The LORD bless you and keep you;
the LORD make his face to shine upon you and be gracious to you;
the LORD lift up his countenance upon you and give you peace.
Numbers 6:24-26

EVENING PRAYER

Call to Prayer

Hear God call you to abide with Him through His Word.

> Jesus said, "Let the little children come to me and do not hinder them, **for to such belongs the kingdom of heaven."** *Matthew 19:14*

Adoration

Delight in the goodness of God.

> I will bless the LORD at all times;
>   his praise shall continually be in my mouth.
> **My soul makes its boast in the LORD;**
>   **let the humble hear and be glad.**
> Oh, magnify the LORD with me,
>   and let us exalt his name together!   *Psalm 34:1-3*

Confession

Confess your sins to God.

Thanksgiving

Give thanks to God.

Psalm

Pray with the people of God in the Psalms.
Psalms 65-67

Scripture Reading

Prayerfully read a portion of God's Word.
Joshua 1 and 24:1-28

Silence

Keep a moment of quiet stillness to listen to God.

Behold, I am the servant of the Lord; let it be to me according to your word. ***Amen.*** *Luke 1:38*

The Lord's Prayer

Pray the words that the Lord Jesus taught His disciples to pray.

Supplication

Earnestly ask God to accomplish His gracious will.

Keep watch, dear Lord, with those who work, or watch, or weep this night, and give thine angles charge over those who sleep. Tend the sick, Lord Christ, give rest to the weary, bless the dying, soothe the suffering, pity the afflicted, shield the joyous, and all for thy love's sake. ***Amen.***

Blessing

Receive God's transforming grace through His Word.

Oh, taste and see that the LORD is good!

Blessed is the man who takes refuge in him! *Psalm 34:8*

DAY 13
FRIDAY

MORNING PRAYER

Call to Prayer

Hear God call you to abide with Him through His Word.

> I call upon you, for you will answer me, O God;
>   incline your ear to me; hear my words.
> **Wondrously show your steadfast love,**
>   **O Savior of those who seek refuge**
>   **from their adversaries at your right hand.**   *Psalm 17:6-7*

Adoration

Delight in the goodness of God.

> I sought the LORD, and he answered me
>   and delivered me from all my fears.
> **Those who look to him are radiant,**
>   **and their faces shall never be ashamed.**
> This poor man cried, and the LORD heard him
>   and saved him out of all his troubles.
> **The angel of the LORD encamps**
>   **around those who fear him, and delivers them.**   *Psalm 34:4-7*

Confession

Confess your sins to God.

> Lord Jesus Christ, great was Your goodness in undertaking my redemption, in consenting to be made sin for me, in conquering all my foes. Great was Your love in manifesting Yourself alive, in showing Your sacred wounds, that every fear might vanish, and every doubt be removed. Great was Your mercy in ascending to heaven, in being crowned and enthroned there to intercede for me, there to help me in temptation, there to open the eternal book, there to receive me finally to Yourself. Great was Your wisdom in devising this means of salvation; bathe my soul in rich consolations of Your resurrection life. O God, pardon all my sins, known and unknown, felt and unfelt, confessed and not confessed, remembered or forgotten. Grant me more and more of the resurrection life: may it rule me, may I walk in its power, and be strengthened through its influence. Amen.

The Valley of Vision: A Collection of Puritan Prayers & Devotions

Thanksgiving

Give thanks to God.

Psalm

Pray with the people of God in the Psalms.
Psalm 68

Scripture Reading

Prayerfully read a portion of God's Word.
Judges 2:11-23 and 1 Samuel 4:1-11

Silence

Keep a moment of quiet stillness to listen to God.

O God of peace, who hast taught us that in returning and rest we shall be saved, in quietness and in confidence shall be our strength: By the might of thy Spirit lift us, we pray thee, to thy presence, where we may be still and know that thou art God, through Jesus Christ our Lord. ***Amen.*** *To Be a Christian: An Anglican Catechism*

The Lord's Prayer

Pray the words that the Lord Jesus taught His disciples to pray.

Supplication

Earnestly ask God to accomplish His gracious will.

Almighty God, whose creation, and the work of whose hands we are— grant us to know that we exist and move in you alone, so that we may submit ourselves unto you, not merely being directed by your secret providence, but showing ourselves your willing and obedient followers, as it becomes sons. Thus may we endeavor to glorify your name in this world, till we arrive at the enjoyment of that blessed heritage which is laid up for us in heaven, through Christ our Lord. ***Amen.*** *John Calvin*

Blessing

Receive God's transforming grace through His Word.

The Lord Jesus said, "But blessed are your eyes, for they see, and your ears, for they hear." *Matthew 13:16*

EVENING PRAYER

Call to Prayer

Hear God call you to abide with Him through His Word.

"The time is fulfilled, **and the kingdom of God is at hand;** repent and believe in the gospel." *Mark 1:15*

Adoration

Delight in the goodness of God.

Let the heavens be glad, and let the earth rejoice;
let the sea roar, and all that fills it;
let the field exult, and everything in it!
Then shall all the trees of the forest sing for joy
before the LORD, for he comes,
for he comes to judge the earth.
He will judge the world in righteousness,
and the peoples in his faithfulness. *Psalm 96:11-13*

Confession

Confess your sins to God.

Thanksgiving

Give thanks to God.

Psalm

Pray with the people of God in the Psalms.
Psalms 69-70

Scripture Reading

Prayerfully read a portion of God's Word.

Judges 2:11-23 and 1 Samuel 4:1-11

Silence

Keep a moment of quiet stillness to listen to God.

Speak, LORD, for your servant hears. ***Amen.*** *1 Samuel 3:9*

The Lord's Prayer

Pray the words that the Lord Jesus taught His disciples to pray.

Supplication

Earnestly ask God to accomplish His gracious will.

O Merciful Lord God, heavenly Father, whether we sleep or wake, live or die, we are always thine. Wherefore I beseech thee heartily to take care and charge of me, not suffering me to perish in the works of darkness, but kindling the light of thy countenance in my heart, that thy godly knowledge may daily increase in me, through a right and pure faith, and that I may always be found to walk and live after thy wisdom and pleasure, through Jesus Christ our Lord and Savior. ***Amen.***

Blessing

Receive God's transforming grace through His Word.

The Lord Jesus said, "Blessed rather are those who hear the word of God and keep it!" *Luke 11:28*

DAY 14

SATURDAY

MORNING PRAYER

Call to Prayer

Hear God call you to abide with Him through His Word.

> Keep me as the apple of your eye;
>> **hide me in the shadow of your wings.** *Psalm 17:8*

Adoration

Delight in the goodness of God.

> The LORD is my chosen portion and my cup;
>> you hold my lot.
> **The lines have fallen for me in pleasant places;**
>> **indeed, I have a beautiful inheritance.** *Psalm 16:5-6*

Confession

Confess your sins to God.

> *Almighty and everlasting God, You hate nothing You have made, and You forgive the sins of all who are penitent: Create and make in us new and contrite hearts, that we, worthily lamenting our sins and acknowledging wretchedness, may obtain of You, the God of all mercy, perfect remission and forgiveness; through Jesus Christ our Lord; who*

lives and reigns with You and the Holy Spirit, one God, for ever and
ever. Amen.   To Be a Christian: An Anglican Catechism

Thanksgiving

Give thanks to God for His grace and daily mercies.

Psalm

Pray with the people of God in the Psalms.
Psalms 71-72

Scripture Reading

Prayerfully read a portion of God's Word.
1 Samuel 8 and 17

Silence

Keep a moment of quiet stillness to listen to God.

> Take our minds, and think through them. Take our lips, and speak
> through them. Take our hearts, and set them on fire with love for thee.
> What we know not, teach us. What we have not, give us. What we are
> not, make us. For Jesus Christ's sake. *Amen.*

The Lord's Prayer

Pray the words that the Lord Jesus taught His disciples to pray.

Supplication

Earnestly ask God to accomplish His gracious will.

> O Lord, who hast brought us through the darkness of night to the light
> of morning, and who by thy Holy Spirit dost illumine the darkness of
> ignorance and sin: We beseech thee of thy loving-kindness to pour thy

holy light into our souls, that we may be ever devoted to thee, by whose wisdom we were created, by whose mercy we were redeemed, and by whose providence we are governed, to the honor and glory of thy great name. *Amen.*

Blessing

Receive God's transforming grace through His Word.

> Surely goodness and mercy shall follow me
> all the days of my life,
> and I shall dwell in the house of the LORD
> forever.   *Psalm 23:6*

EVENING PRAYER

Call to Prayer

Hear God call you to abide with Him through His Word.

First of all, then, I urge that supplications, prayers, intercessions, and thanksgivings be made for all people, *for kings and all who are in high positions, that we may lead a peaceful and quiet life, godly and dignified in every way.* This is good, and it is pleasing in the sight of God our Savior, *who desires all people to be saved and to come to the knowledge of the truth.*   *1 Timothy 2:1-4*

Adoration

Delight in the goodness of God.

Therefore my heart is glad, and my whole being rejoices;
  my flesh also dwells secure.
For you will not abandon my soul to Sheol,
  or let your holy one see corruption.
You make known to me the path of life;
  in your presence there is fullness of joy;
    at your right hand are pleasures forevermore.   *Psalm 16:9-11*

Confession

Confess your sins to God.

Thanksgiving

Give thanks to God for His grace and daily mercies.

Psalm

Pray with the people of God in the Psalms.
Psalms 73-74

Scripture Reading

Prayerfully read a portion of God's Word.

1 Samuel 8 and 17

Silence

Keep a moment of quiet stillness to listen to God.

> For God alone my soul waits in silence;
> from him comes my salvation.
> He only is my rock and my salvation,
> my fortress; I shall not be greatly moved. **Amen.**   *Psalm 62:1-2*

The Lord's Prayer

Pray the words that the Lord Jesus taught His disciples to pray.

Supplication

Earnestly ask God to accomplish His gracious will.

> O God, from whom all holy desires, all good counsels, and all just works do proceed: Give unto thy servants that peace which the world cannot give; that both our hearts may be set to obey thy commandments, and also that by thee we being defended from the fear of our enemies may pass our time in rest and quietness; through the merits of Jesus Christ our Savior. **Amen.**   *The 1662 Book of Common Prayer*

Blessing

Receive God's transforming grace through His Word.

> As they were talking about these things, Jesus himself stood among them, and said to them, "Peace to you!"   *Luke 24:36*

DAY 15
THE THIRD SUNDAY IN ADVENT

MORNING PRAYER

Call to Prayer

Hear God call you to abide with Him through His Word.

> O LORD, my heart is not lifted up;
>   my eyes are not raised too high;
> **I do not occupy myself with things**
>   **too great and too marvelous for me.**
> But I have calmed and quieted my soul,
>   like a weaned child with its mother;
>   like a weaned child is my soul within me.
> **O Israel, hope in the LORD**
>   **from this time forth and forevermore.**   *Psalm 131:1-3*

Adoration

Delight in the goodness of God.

> Worthy are you to take the scroll
>   and to open its seals,
> **for you were slain, and by your blood you ransomed people for God**
>   **from every tribe and language and people and nation,**
> and you have made them a kingdom and priests to our God,
>   and they shall reign on the earth.   *Revelation 5:9-10*

Confession

Confess your sins to God.

> *Have mercy on me, O God,*
> *according to Your steadfast love;*
> *according to Your abundant mercy*
> *blot out my transgressions.*
> *Wash me thoroughly from my iniquity,*
> *and cleanse me from my sin! . . .*
> *Restore to me the joy of your salvation,*
> *and uphold me with a willing spirit. Amen. Psalm 51:1-2, 12*

Thanksgiving

Give thanks to God for His grace and daily mercies.

Psalm

Pray with the people of God in the Psalms.
Psalms 75-77

Scripture Reading

Prayerfully read a portion of God's Word.
Micah 5:2-5

Silence

Keep a moment of quiet stillness to listen to God.

> Fix our hearts on thee, O God, in pure devotion, that the vain pursuits of
> this world may have no hold upon us, and that we may be changed, by the
> consuming fire of thy Spirit, into the image and likeness of thy Son, Jesus
> Christ our Lord, to whom, with thee and the same Spirit, be an honor
> and glory, world without end. ***Amen.***

The Lord's Prayer

Pray the words that the Lord Jesus taught His disciples to pray.

Supplication

Earnestly ask God to accomplish His gracious will.

> Almighty God, give us grace that we may cast away the works of darkness, and put upon us the armor of light, now in the time of this mortal life, in which thy Son Jesus Christ came to visit us in great humility, that in the last day, when he shall come again in his glorious majesty, to judge both the quick and the dead, we may rise to the life immortal, through him who liveth and reigneth with thee and the Holy Ghost, now and forever. ***Amen.***
> *The 1662 Book of Common Prayer*

Blessing

Receive God's transforming grace through His Word.

> Jesus said to him, "Have you believed because you have seen me? Blessed are those who have not seen and yet have believed." *John 20:29*

EVENING PRAYER

Call to Prayer

Hear God call you to abide with Him through His Word.

And Jesus said to him, "What do you want me to do for you?" ***And the blind man said to him, "Rabbi, let me recover my sight."*** And Jesus said to him, "Go your way; your faith has made you well." *Mark 10:51-52*

Adoration

Delight in the goodness of God.

Worthy is the Lamb who was slain,

to receive power and wealth and wisdom and might and honor and glory and blessing! *Revelation 5:12*

Confession

Confess your sins to God.

Thanksgiving

Give thanks to God for His grace and daily mercies.

Psalm

Pray with the people of God in the Psalms.
Psalm 78

Scripture Reading

Prayerfully read a portion of God's Word.
Micah 5:2-5

Silence

Keep a moment of quiet stillness to listen to God.

Behold, I am the servant of the Lord; let it be to me according to your word. ***Amen.*** *Luke 1:38*

The Lord's Prayer

Pray the words that the Lord Jesus taught His disciples to pray.

Supplication

Earnestly ask God to accomplish His gracious will.

Answer me when I call, O God of my righteousness!
 You have given me relief when I was in distress.
 Be gracious to me and hear my prayer! . . .
In peace I will both lie down and sleep;
 for You alone, O LORD, make me dwell in safety. ***Amen.*** *Psalm 4:1, 8*

Blessing

Receive God's transforming grace through His Word.

The God of peace will soon crush Satan under your feet. The grace of our Lord Jesus Christ be with you. *Romans 16:20*

DAY 16
MONDAY

MORNING PRAYER

Call to Prayer

Hear God call you to abide with Him through His Word.

> The LORD your God is in your midst,
>   a mighty one who will save;
> ***he will rejoice over you with gladness;***
>   ***he will quiet you by his love;***
> he will exult over you with loud singing.   *Zephaniah 3:17*

Adoration

Delight in the goodness of God.

> To him who sits on the throne and to the Lamb
> ***be blessing and honor and glory and might forever and ever!***
> *Revelation 5:13*

Confession

Confess your sins to God.

> ***O Lord, You have mercy upon all—take away from me my sins, and
> mercifully kindle in me the fire of Your Holy Spirit. Take away from me
> the heart of stone, and give me a heart of flesh, a heart to love and adore***

You, a heart to delight in You, to follow and to enjoy You, for Christ's
sake. Amen.   Ambrose

Thanksgiving
Give thanks to God for His grace and daily mercies.

Psalm
Pray with the people of God in the Psalms.
Psalms 79-81

Scripture Reading
Prayerfully read a portion of God's Word.
2 Samuel 7 and Psalm 51

Silence
Keep a moment of quiet stillness to listen to God.

> O God of peace, who hast taught us that in returning and rest we shall be
> saved, in quietness and in confidence shall be our strength: By the might
> of thy Spirit lift us, we pray thee, to thy presence, where we may be still
> and know that thou art God, through Jesus Christ our Lord. *Amen.*
> *To Be a Christian: An Anglican Catechism*

The Lord's Prayer
Pray the words that the Lord Jesus taught His disciples to pray.

Supplication
Earnestly ask God to accomplish His gracious will.

> Incline us, O God, to think humbly of ourselves, to be severe only in the
> examination of our own conduct, to consider our fellow-creatures with

kindness, and to judge of all they say and do with that charity which we would desire from them ourselves. Grant this most merciful Father, for the sake of our blessed Savior, who hast set us an example of such a temper of forbearance and patience, to whom with thee and the Holy Ghost be all honor and glory, world without end. ***Amen.***

Blessing

Receive God's transforming grace through His Word.

The sting of death is sin, and the power of sin is the law. But thanks be to God, who gives us the victory through our Lord Jesus Christ.

Therefore, my beloved brothers, be steadfast, immovable, always abounding in the work of the Lord, knowing that in the Lord your labor is not in vain. *1 Corinthians 15:56-68*

EVENING PRAYER

Call to Prayer

Hear God call you to abide with Him through His Word.

Humble yourselves, therefore, under the mighty hand of God so that at the proper time he may exalt you, **casting all your anxieties on him, because he cares for you.**   *1 Peter 5:6-7*

Adoration

Delight in the goodness of God.

Bless the LORD, O my soul,
  and all that is within me,
    bless his holy name!
**Bless the LORD, O my soul,
  and forget not all his benefits,**
who forgives all your iniquity,
  who heals all your diseases,
*who redeems your life from the pit,
  who crowns you with steadfast love and mercy,*
who satisfies you with good
  so that your youth is renewed like the eagle's.   *Psalm 103:1-5*

Confession

Confess your sins to God.

Thanksgiving

Give thanks to God for His grace and daily mercies.

Psalm

Pray with the people of God in the Psalms.

Psalms 82-85

Scripture Reading

Prayerfully read a portion of God's Word.

2 Samuel 7 and Psalm 51

Silence

Keep a moment of quiet stillness to listen to God.

> Speak, LORD, for your servant hears. *Amen. 1 Samuel 3:9*

The Lord's Prayer

Pray the words that the Lord Jesus taught His disciples to pray.

Supplication

Earnestly ask God to accomplish His gracious will.

> Lighten our darkness, we beseech thee, O Lord; and by thy great mercy
> defend us from all perils and dangers of this night; for the love of thy only
> Son, our Savior, Jesus Christ. *Amen.*
> *The 1662 Book of Common Prayer*

Blessing

Receive God's transforming grace through His Word.

> The grace of the Lord Jesus Christ and the love of God and the fellowship
> of the Holy Spirit be with you all. *2 Corinthians 13:14*

DAY 17

TUESDAY

MORNING PRAYER

Call to Prayer

Hear God call you to abide with Him through His Word.

> Hear my prayer, O LORD;
> **let my cry come to you!**   *Psalm 102:1*

Adoration

Delight in the goodness of God.

> Holy, holy, holy is the LORD of hosts;
> **the whole earth is full of his glory!**   *Isaiah 6:3*

Confession

Confess your sins to God.

> **Cleanse me from my secret faults, O Lord, and forgive those offenses to Your servant which he has caused in others. I contend not in judgment with You, who are truth; I fear to deceive myself, lest my sin should make me think that I am not sinful. Therefore, I contend not in judgment with You; for if You, Lord, should mark iniquities, O Lord, who shall abide? Amen.**   *Augustine*

Thanksgiving

Give thanks to God for His grace and daily mercies.

Psalm

Pray with the people of God in the Psalms.

Psalms 86-88

Scripture Reading

Prayerfully read a portion of God's Word.

1 Kings 3 and 8:1-21

Silence

Keep a moment of quiet stillness to listen to God.

> Take our minds, and think through them. Take our lips, and speak through them. Take our hearts, and set them on fire with love for thee. What we know not, teach us. What we have not, give us. What we are not, make us. For Jesus Christ's sake. ***Amen.***

The Lord's Prayer

Pray the words that the Lord Jesus taught His disciples to pray.

Supplication

Earnestly ask God to accomplish His gracious will.

> O most loving Father, who willest us to give thanks for all things, to dread nothing but the loss of thee, and to cast all our care on thee, who carest for us: Preserve us from faithless fears and worldly anxieties, and grant that no clouds of this mortal life may hide us from the light of that love which is immortal, and which thou has manifested unto us in thy Son, Jesus Christ our Lord. ***Amen.***

Blessing

Receive God's transforming grace through His Word.

Peace be to the brothers, and love with faith, from God the Father and the Lord Jesus Christ. Grace be with all who love our Lord Jesus Christ with love incorruptible. *Ephesians 6:23-24*

EVENING PRAYER

Call to Prayer

Hear God call you to abide with Him through His Word.

> If any of you lacks wisdom, let him ask God, **who gives generously to all without reproach**, and it will be given him.   *James 1:5*

Adoration

Delight in the goodness of God.

> Sing praises to the LORD, O you his saints,
>   and give thanks to his holy name.
> **For his anger is but for a moment,**
>   **and his favor is for a lifetime.**
> Weeping may tarry for the night,
>   but joy comes with the morning.   *Psalm 30:4-5*

Confession

Confess your sins to God.

Thanksgiving

Give thanks to God for His grace and daily mercies.

Psalm

Pray with the people of God in the Psalms.
Psalm 89

Scripture Reading

Prayerfully read a portion of God's Word.
1 Kings 3 and 8:1-21

Silence

Keep a moment of quiet stillness to listen to God.

> For God alone my soul waits in silence;
> from him comes my salvation.
> He only is my rock and my salvation,
> my fortress; I shall not be greatly moved. ***Amen.*** *Psalm 62:1-2*

The Lord's Prayer

Pray the words that the Lord Jesus taught His disciples to pray.

Supplication

Earnestly ask God to accomplish His gracious will.

> But you, O LORD, are a shield about me,
> my glory, and the lifter of my head.
> I cried aloud to the LORD,
> and he answered me from his holy hill. *Psalm 3:3-4*

Blessing

Receive God's transforming grace through His Word.

> The grace of the Lord Jesus Christ be with your spirit. *Philippians 4:23*

DAY 18
WEDNESDAY

MORNING PRAYER

Call to Prayer

Hear God call you to abide with Him through His Word.

> To you, O LORD, I lift up my soul.
> **O my God, in you I trust;**
>   let me not be put to shame;
>   **let not my enemies exult over me.**   *Psalm 25:1-2*

Adoration

Delight in the goodness of God.

> Your words were found, and I ate them,
>   **and your words became to me a joy**
>   **and the delight of my heart,**
> for I am called by your name,
>   O LORD, God of hosts.   *Jeremiah 15:16*

Confession

Confess your sins to God.

> **O Lord my God, light of the blind, and strength of the weak; yes, also**
> **light of those that see, and strength of the strong—hearken unto my**

soul, and hear it crying out of the depths. Woe is me! . . . Lord, help us to turn and seek You; for not as we have forsaken our Creator have You forsaken Your creation. Let us turn and seek You, for we know You are here in our heart, when we confess to You, when we cast ourselves upon You, and weep in Your bosom, after all our rugged ways; and You gently wipe away our tears, and we weep the more for joy; because You, Lord—not man of flesh and blood—but You, Lord, who made us, remake and comfort us. Amen.   *Augustine*

Thanksgiving
Give thanks to God for His grace and daily mercies.

Psalm
Pray with the people of God in the Psalms.
Psalms 90-92

Scripture Reading
Prayerfully read a portion of God's Word.
1 Kings 18:16-40 and 2 Kings 17:1-18

Silence
Keep a moment of quiet stillness to listen to God.

Fix our hearts on thee, O God, in pure devotion, that the vain pursuits of this world may have no hold upon us, and that we may be changed, by the consuming fire of thy Spirit, into the image and likeness of thy Son, Jesus Christ our Lord, to whom, with thee and the same Spirit, be an honor and glory, world without end. *Amen.*

The Lord's Prayer

Pray the words that the Lord Jesus taught His disciples to pray.

Supplication

Earnestly ask God to accomplish His gracious will.

> O God, whose arm is mighty to save: Uphold and deliver all those who suffer for Thy name, bearing in their bodies the dying of our Lord Jesus, and as they have known the fellowship of His sufferings, make them to know the power of His resurrection, through the same Jesus Christ our Lord. ***Amen.***

Blessing

Receive God's transforming grace through His Word.

> "In overflowing anger for a moment
>   I hid my face from you,
> but with everlasting love I will have compassion on you,"
>   says the LORD, your Redeemer.   *Isaiah 54:8*

EVENING PRAYER

Call to Prayer

Hear God call you to abide with Him through His Word.

> Consequently, he is able to save to the uttermost those who draw near to God through him, ***since he always lives to make intercession for them.***
> *Hebrews 7:25*

Adoration

Delight in the goodness of God.

> Praise the LORD!
> ***Praise God in his sanctuary;***
> ***praise him in his mighty heavens!***
> Praise him for his mighty deeds;
> praise him according to his excellent greatness!   *Psalm 150:1-2*

Confession

Confess your sins to God.

Thanksgiving

Give thanks to God for His grace and daily mercies.

Psalm

Pray with the people of God in the Psalms.
Psalms 93-94

Scripture Reading

Prayerfully read a portion of God's Word.
1 Kings 18:16-40 and 2 Kings 17:1-18

Silence

Keep a moment of quiet stillness to listen to God.

> Behold, I am the servant of the Lord; let it be to me according to your word. ***Amen.*** *Luke 1:38*

The Lord's Prayer

Pray the words that the Lord Jesus taught His disciples to pray.

Supplication

Earnestly ask God to accomplish His gracious will.

> As a reconciled Father, take me to be your child; and give me your renewing Spirit, to be in me a principle of holy life, and light, and love, and your seal and witness that I am yours. Let him quicken my dead and hardened heart. Let him enlighten my dark and unbelieving mind, by clearer knowledge and firm belief. Let him turn my will to the ready obedience of your holy will. Let him reveal to my soul the wonders of your love in Christ, and fill it with love to you and my Redeemer, and to all your holy Word and works. ***Amen.*** *Richard Baxter*

Blessing

Receive God's transforming grace through His Word.

> The Lord Jesus said, "Sanctify them in the truth; your word is truth. As you sent me into the world, so I have sent them into the world. And for their sake I consecrate myself, that they also may be sanctified in truth. *John 17:17-19*

DAY 19
THURSDAY

MORNING PRAYER

Call to Prayer

Hear God call you to abide with Him through His Word.

> I rise before dawn and cry for help;
>> ***I hope in your words.*** *Psalm 119:147*

Adoration

Delight in the goodness of God.

> I will give thanks to the LORD with my whole heart;
>> ***I will recount all of your wonderful deeds.***
> I will be glad and exult in you;
>> ***I will sing praise to your name, O Most High.*** *Psalm 9:1-2*

Confession

Confess your sins to God.

> ***O You plenteous source of every good and perfect gift, shed abroad the cheering light of Your sevenfold grace over our hearts. Yes, Spirit of love and gentleness, we most humbly implore Your assistance. You know our faults, our failings, our necessities, the dullness of our understanding, the waywardness of our affections, the perverseness of our will. When,***

therefore, we neglect to practice what we know, visit us, we ask You, with Your grace; enlighten our minds, rectify our desires, correct our wanderings, and pardon our omissions, so that by Your guidance we may be preserved from making shipwreck of faith, and keep a good conscience, and may at length be landed safe in the haven of eternal rest; through Jesus Christ our Lord. Amen.   Anselm

Thanksgiving
Give thanks to God for His grace and daily mercies.

Psalm
Pray with the people of God in the Psalms.
Psalms 95-97

Scripture Reading
Prayerfully read a portion of God's Word.
2 Kings 24-25 and Jeremiah 7:1-15

Silence
Keep a moment of quiet stillness to listen to God.

O God of peace, who hast taught us that in returning and rest we shall be saved, in quietness and in confidence shall be our strength: By the might of thy Spirit lift us, we pray thee, to thy presence, where we may be still and know that thou art God, through Jesus Christ our Lord. **Amen.**
To Be a Christian: An Anglican Catechism

The Lord's Prayer

Pray the words that the Lord Jesus taught His disciples to pray.

Supplication

Earnestly ask God to accomplish His gracious will.

O most merciful Father, we humbly thank thee for all thy gifts so freely bestowed upon us. For life and health and safety, for power to work and leisure to rest, for all that is beautiful in creation and in the lives of men, we praise and magnify thy holy name. But above all, we thank thee for our spiritual mercies in Christ Jesus our Lord, for the means of grace, and for the hope of glory. Fill our hearts with all joy and peace in believing, through Jesus Christ our Lord. ***Amen.***

Blessing

Receive God's transforming grace through His Word.

The Lord Jesus said, "I do not ask for these only, but also for those who will believe in me through their word, that they may all be one, just as you, Father, are in me, and I in you, that they also may be in us, so that the world may believe that you have sent me."   *John 17:20-21*

EVENING PRAYER

Call to Prayer

Hear God call you to abide with Him through His Word.

Likewise the Spirit helps us in our weakness. ***For we do not know what to pray for as we ought, but the Spirit himself intercedes for us with groanings too deep for words.*** And he who searches hearts knows what is the mind of the Spirit, ***because the Spirit intercedes for the saints according to the will of God.*** Romans 8:26-27

Adoration

Delight in the goodness of God.

When the LORD restored the fortunes of Zion,
  we were like those who dream.
Then our mouth was filled with laughter,
  and our tongue with shouts of joy;
then they said among the nations,
  "The LORD has done great things for them."
The LORD has done great things for us;
  we are glad.
Restore our fortunes, O LORD,
  like streams in the Negeb!
Those who sow in tears
  shall reap with shouts of joy!
He who goes out weeping,
  bearing the seed for sowing,

shall come home with shouts of joy,
  bringing his sheaves with him.   Psalm 126:1-6

Confession

Confess your sins to God.

Thanksgiving

Give thanks to God for His grace and daily mercies.

Psalm

Pray with the people of God in the Psalms.
Psalms 98-101

Scripture Reading

Prayerfully read a portion of God's Word.
2 Kings 24-25 and Jeremiah 7:1-15

Silence

Keep a moment of quiet stillness to listen to God.

Speak, LORD, for your servant hears. ***Amen***. *1 Samuel 3:9*

The Lord's Prayer

Pray the words that the Lord Jesus taught His disciples to pray.

Supplication

Earnestly ask God to accomplish His gracious will.

Keep watch, dear Lord, with those who work, or watch, or weep this night, and give thine angels charge over those who sleep. Tend the sick, Lord Christ, give rest to the weary, bless the dying, soothe the suffering, pity the afflicted, shield the joyous, and all for thy love's sake. ***Amen.***

Blessing

Receive God's transforming grace through His Word.

> Blessed is everyone who fears the LORD,
>> who walks in his ways!
> You shall eat the fruit of the labor of your hands;
>> you shall be blessed, and it shall be well with you. *Psalm 128:1-2*

DAY 20
FRIDAY

MORNING PRAYER

Call to Prayer

Hear God call you to abide with Him through His Word.

> I wait for the LORD, my soul waits,
>> **and in his word I hope;**
> my soul waits for the LORD
>> **more than watchmen for the morning,**
>> **more than watchmen for the morning.**   *Psalm 130:5-6*

Adoration

Delight in the goodness of God.

> The LORD is gracious and merciful,
>> slow to anger and abounding in steadfast love.
> **The LORD is good to all,**
>> **and his mercy is over all that he has made.**   *Psalm 145:8-9*

Confession

Confess your sins to God.

> *Lord Jesus Christ, great was Your goodness in undertaking my redemption, in consenting to be made sin for me, in conquering all*

my foes. Great was Your love in manifesting Yourself alive, in showing Your sacred wounds, that every fear might vanish, and every doubt be removed. Great was Your mercy in ascending to heaven, in being crowned and enthroned there to intercede for me, there to help me in temptation, there to open the eternal book, there to receive me finally to Yourself. Great was Your wisdom in devising this means of salvation; bathe my soul in rich consolations of Your resurrection life. O God, pardon all my sins, known and unknown, felt and unfelt, confessed and not confessed, remembered or forgotten. Grant me more and more of the resurrection life: may it rule me, may I walk in its power, and be strengthened through its influence. Amen.

The Valley of Vision: A Collection of Puritan Prayers & Devotions

Thanksgiving

Give thanks to God for His grace and daily mercies.

Psalm

Pray with the people of God in the Psalms.

Psalms 102-103

Scripture Reading

Prayerfully read a portion of God's Word.

Psalm 137:1-6 and Haggai 1

Silence

Keep a moment of quiet stillness to listen to God.

Take our minds, and think through them. Take our lips, and speak through them. Take our hearts, and set them on fire with love for thee. What we know not, teach us. What we have not, give us. What we are not, make us. For Jesus Christ's sake. ***Amen.***

The Lord's Prayer

Pray the words that the Lord Jesus taught His disciples to pray.

Supplication

Earnestly ask God to accomplish His gracious will.

O Lord, our Savior, You have warned us that You will require much of those to whom much is given—grant that we whose lot is cast in so goodly a heritage may strive together the more abundantly to extend to others what we so richly enjoy; and as we have entered into the labors of other people, so to labor that in their turn other people may enter into ours, to the fulfillment of your holy will. **Amen.** *Augustine*

Blessing

Receive God's transforming grace through His Word.

May the Lord direct your hearts to the love of God and to the steadfastness of Christ. *2 Thessalonians 3:5*

EVENING PRAYER

Call to Prayer

Hear God call you to abide with Him through His Word.

Out of the depths I cry to you, O LORD!
O LORD, hear my voice!
Let your ears be attentive
to the voice of my pleas for mercy!   *Psalm 130:1-2*

Adoration

Delight in the goodness of God.

All your works shall give thanks to you, O LORD,
and all your saints shall bless you!
They shall speak of the glory of your kingdom
and tell of your power,
to make known to the children of man your mighty deeds,
and the glorious splendor of your kingdom.
Your kingdom is an everlasting kingdom,
and your dominion endures throughout all generations. *Psalm 145:10-13*

Confession

Confess your sins to God.

Thanksgiving

Give thanks to God for His grace and daily mercies.

Psalm

Pray with the people of God in the Psalms.

Psalm 104

Scripture Reading

Prayerfully read a portion of God's Word.

Psalm 137:1-6 and Haggai 1

Silence

Keep a moment of quiet stillness to listen to God.

> For God alone my soul waits in silence;
>> from him comes my salvation.
> He only is my rock and my salvation,
>> my fortress; I shall not be greatly moved. ***Amen.*** *Psalm 62:1-2*

The Lord's Prayer

Pray the words that the Lord Jesus taught His disciples to pray.

Supplication

Earnestly ask God to accomplish His gracious will.

> O Merciful Lord God, heavenly Father, whether we sleep or wake, live or die, we are always thine. Wherefore I beseech thee heartily to take care and charge of me, not suffering me to perish in the works of darkness, but kindling the light of thy countenance in my heart, that thy godly knowledge may daily increase in me, through a right and pure faith, and that I may always be found to walk and live after thy wisdom and pleasure, through Jesus Christ our Lord and Savior. ***Amen.***

Blessing

Receive God's transforming grace through His Word.

> Now may the Lord of peace himself give you peace at all times in every way. The Lord be with you all. *2 Thessalonians 3:16*

DAY 21

SATURDAY

MORNING PRAYER

Call to Prayer

Hear God call you to abide with Him through His Word.

> It is good to give thanks to the LORD,
> to sing praises to your name, O Most High;
> **to declare your steadfast love in the morning,**
> **and your faithfulness by night.**   *Psalm 92:1-2*

Adoration

Delight in the goodness of God.

> My lips will shout for joy,
> **when I sing praises to you;**
> my soul also, which you have redeemed.   *Psalm 71:23*

Confession

Confess your sins to God.

> *Almighty and everlasting God, You hate nothing You have made, and You forgive the sins of all who are penitent: Create and make in us new and contrite hearts, that we, worthily lamenting our sins and acknowledging wretchedness, may obtain of You, the God of all mercy,*

perfect remission and forgiveness; through Jesus Christ our Lord; who lives and reigns with You and the Holy Spirit, one God, for ever and ever. Amen.   To Be a Christian: An Anglican Catechism

Thanksgiving

Give thanks to God for His grace and daily mercies.

Psalm

Pray with the people of God in the Psalms.

Psalm 105

Scripture Reading

Prayerfully read a portion of God's Word.

Isaiah 40

Silence

Keep a moment of quiet stillness to listen to God.

Fix our hearts on thee, O God, in pure devotion, that the vain pursuits of this world may have no hold upon us, and that we may be changed, by the consuming fire of thy Spirit, into the image and likeness of thy Son, Jesus Christ our Lord, to whom, with thee and the same Spirit, be an honor and glory, world without end. ***Amen.***

The Lord's Prayer

Pray the words that the Lord Jesus taught His disciples to pray.

Supplication

Earnestly ask God to accomplish His gracious will.

O Lord, who hast brought us through the darkness of night to the light of morning, and who by thy Holy Spirit dost illumine the darkness of ignorance and sin: We beseech thee of thy loving-kindness to pour thy holy light into our souls, that we may be ever devoted to thee, by whose wisdom we were created, by whose mercy we were redeemed, and by whose providence we are governed, to the honor and glory of thy great name. *Amen.*

Blessing

Receive God's transforming grace through His Word.

The Lord be with your spirit. Grace be with you.   *2 Timothy 4:22*

EVENING PRAYER

Call to Prayer

Hear God call you to abide with Him through His Word.

> The Lord Jesus said, "Therefore I tell you, whatever you ask in prayer, believe that you have received it, and it will be yours. And whenever you stand praying, forgive, if you have anything against anyone, so that your Father also who is in heaven may forgive you your trespasses."
> *Mark 11:24-25*

Adoration

Delight in the goodness of God.

Confession

Confess your sins to God.

Thanksgiving

Give thanks to God for His grace and daily mercies.

Psalm

Pray with the people of God in the Psalms.
Psalm 106

Scripture Reading

Prayerfully read a portion of God's Word.
Isaiah 40

Silence

Keep a moment of quiet stillness to listen to God.

> Behold, I am the servant of the Lord; let it be to me according to your word. ***Amen.*** *Luke 1:38*

The Lord's Prayer

Pray the words that the Lord Jesus taught His disciples to pray.

Supplication

Earnestly ask God to accomplish His gracious will.

> O God, from whom all holy desires, all good counsels, and all just works do proceed: Give unto thy servants that peace which the world cannot give; that both our hearts may be set to obey thy commandments, and also that by thee we being defended from the fear of our enemies may pass our time in rest and quietness; through the merits of Jesus Christ our Savior. ***Amen.*** *The 1662 Book of Common Prayer*

Blessing

Receive God's transforming grace through His Word.

> Now may the God of peace who brought again from the dead our Lord Jesus, the great shepherd of the sheep, by the blood of the eternal covenant, equip you with everything good that you may do his will, working in us that which is pleasing in his sight, through Jesus Christ, to whom be glory forever and ever. ***Amen.*** *Hebrews 13:20-21*

DAY 22

THE FOURTH SUNDAY IN ADVENT

MORNING PRAYER

Call to Prayer

Hear God call you to abide with Him through His Word.

> *Fear not, for I am with you;*
> *be not dismayed, for I am your God;*
> **I will strengthen you, I will help you,**
> **I will uphold you with my righteous right hand.**   *Isaiah 41:10*

Adoration

Delight in the goodness of God.

> Blessed are you, O LORD, the God of Israel our father, forever and ever. **Yours, O LORD, is the greatness and the power and the glory and the victory and the majesty, for all that is in the heavens and in the earth is yours.** Yours is the kingdom, O LORD, and you are exalted as head above all. **Both riches and honor come from you, and you rule over all. In your hand are power and might, and in your hand it is to make great and to give strength to all.** And now we thank you, our God, and praise your glorious name.   *1 Chronicles 29:10-13*

Confession

Confess your sins to God.

> **Have mercy on me, O God,**
> **according to Your steadfast love;**
> **according to Your abundant mercy**
> **blot out my transgressions.**
> **Wash me thoroughly from my iniquity,**
> **and cleanse me from my sin!** . . .
> **Restore to me the joy of your salvation,**
> **and uphold me with a willing spirit. Amen.** *Psalm 51:1-2, 12*

Thanksgiving

Give thanks to God for His grace and daily mercies.

Psalm

Pray with the people of God in the Psalms.
Psalm 107

Scripture Reading

Prayerfully read a portion of God's Word.
Malachi 4 and Luke 1:5-25, 57-80

Silence

Keep a moment of quiet stillness to listen to God.

> O God of peace, who hast taught us that in returning and rest we shall
> be saved, in quietness and in confidence shall be our strength: By the
> might of thy Spirit lift us, we pray thee, to thy presence, where we may be
> still and know that thou art God, through Jesus Christ our Lord. ***Amen.***
> *To Be a Christian: An Anglican Catechism*

The Lord's Prayer

Pray the words that the Lord Jesus taught His disciples to pray.

Supplication

Earnestly ask God to accomplish His gracious will.

> Almighty God, give us grace that we may cast away the works of darkness, and put upon us the armor of light, now in the time of this mortal life, in which thy Son Jesus Christ came to visit us in great humility, that in the last day, when he shall come again in his glorious majesty, to judge both the quick and the dead, we may rise to the life immortal, through him who liveth and reigneth with thee and the Holy Ghost, now and forever. ***Amen.***   *The 1662 Book of Common Prayer*

Blessing

Receive God's transforming grace through His Word.

> Blessed be the God and Father of our Lord Jesus Christ! According to his great mercy, he has caused us to be born again to a living hope through the resurrection of Jesus Christ from the dead, to an inheritance that is imperishable, undefiled, and unfading, kept in heaven for you, who by God's power are being guarded through faith for a salvation ready to be revealed in the last time.   *1 Peter 1:3-5*

EVENING PRAYER

Call to Prayer

Hear God call you to abide with Him through His Word.

The Lord Jesus said, "Come to me, all who labor and are heavy laden, and I will give you rest. ***Take my yoke upon you, and learn from me, for I am gentle and lowly in heart,*** and you will find rest for your souls. ***For my yoke is easy, and my burden is light.***" *Matthew 11:28-30*

Adoration

Delight in the goodness of God.

O LORD, God of Israel, there is no God like you, in heaven above or on earth beneath, ***keeping covenant and showing steadfast love to your servants who walk before you with all their heart.*** *1 Kings 8:23*

Confession

Confess your sins to God.

Thanksgiving

Give thanks to God for His grace and daily mercies.

Psalm

Pray with the people of God in the Psalms.
Psalms 108-109

Scripture Reading

Prayerfully read a portion of God's Word.
Malachi 4 and Luke 1:5-25, 57-80

Silence

Keep a moment of quiet stillness to listen to God.

> Speak, LORD, for your servant hears. ***Amen****. 1 Samuel 3:9*

The Lord's Prayer

Pray the words that the Lord Jesus taught His disciples to pray.

Supplication

Earnestly ask God to accomplish His gracious will.

> Answer me when I call, O God of my righteousness!
>> You have given me relief when I was in distress.
>> Be gracious to me and hear my prayer! . . .
> In peace I will both lie down and sleep;
>> for you alone, O LORD, make me dwell in safety. ***Amen****. Psalm 4:1, 8*

Blessing

Receive God's transforming grace through His Word.

> He who testifies to these things says, "Surely I am coming soon." ***Amen***.
> Come, Lord Jesus!
> The grace of the Lord Jesus be with all. ***Amen****. Revelation 22:20-21*

DAY 23

MONDAY

MORNING PRAYER

Call to Prayer

Hear God call you to abide with Him through His Word.

> To you I lift up my eyes,
>> O You who are enthroned in the heavens!
>> **Behold, as the eyes of servants**
>>> **look to the hand of their master,**
>> as the eyes of a maidservant
>>> to the hand of her mistress,
>> **so our eyes look to the LORD our God,**
>>> **till he has mercy upon us.**   *Psalm 123:1-2*

Adoration

Delight in the goodness of God.

> O LORD, our Lord,
>> **how majestic is your name in all the earth!**   *Psalm 8:9*

Confession

Confess your sins to God.

> **O Lord, You have mercy upon all—take away from me my sins, and mercifully kindle in me the fire of Your Holy Spirit. Take away from me**

the heart of stone, and give me a heart of flesh, a heart to love and adore You, a heart to delight in You, to follow and to enjoy You, for Christ's sake. Amen.   Ambrose

Thanksgiving

Give thanks to God for His grace and daily mercies.

Psalm

Pray with the people of God in the Psalms.

Psalms 110-113

Scripture Reading

Prayerfully read a portion of God's Word.

Luke 1:26-38

Silence

Keep a moment of quiet stillness to listen to God.

Take our minds, and think through them. Take our lips, and speak through them. Take our hearts, and set them on fire with love for thee. What we know not, teach us. What we have not, give us. What we are not, make us. For Jesus Christ's sake. *Amen.*

The Lord's Prayer

Pray the words that the Lord Jesus taught His disciples to pray.

Supplication

Earnestly ask God to accomplish His gracious will.

O Heavenly Father, who hast filled the world with beauty: Open, we beseech thee, our eyes to behold thy gracious hand in all thy works, that, rejoicing in thy whole creation, we may learn to serve thee with gladness, for the sake of him by whom all things were made, thy Son, Jesus Christ our Lord. ***Amen.***

Blessing

Receive God's transforming grace through His Word.

> The LORD bless you and keep you;
> the LORD make his face to shine upon you and be gracious to you;
> the LORD lift up his countenance upon you and give you peace.
> *Numbers 6:24-26*

EVENING PRAYER

Call to Prayer

Hear God call you to abide with Him through His Word.

> Jesus turned and saw them following and said to them, "What are you seeking?" **And they said to him, "Rabbi" (which means Teacher),** **"where are you staying?"** He said to them, "Come and you will see." *John 1:38-39*

Adoration

Delight in the goodness of God.

> Great and amazing are Your deeds,
>   O LORD God the Almighty!
> **Just and true are your ways,**
>   **O King of the nations!**
> Who will not fear, O LORD,
>   and glorify your name?
> **For you alone are holy.**
>   All nations will come
>   and worship you,
> **for your righteous acts have been revealed.** *Revelation 15:3-4*

Confession

Confess your sins to God.

Thanksgiving

Give thanks to God for His grace and daily mercies.

Psalm

Pray with the people of God in the Psalms.

Psalms 114-115

Scripture Reading

Prayerfully read a portion of God's Word.

Luke 1:26-38

Silence

Keep a moment of quiet stillness to listen to God.

> For God alone my soul waits in silence;
>> from him comes my salvation.
> He only is my rock and my salvation,
>> my fortress; I shall not be greatly moved. ***Amen.*** *Psalm 62:1-2*

The Lord's Prayer

Pray the words that the Lord Jesus taught His disciples to pray.

Supplication

Earnestly ask God to accomplish His gracious will.

> Lighten our darkness, we beseech thee, O Lord; and by thy great mercy defend us from all perils and dangers of this night; for the love of thy only Son, our Savior, Jesus Christ. ***Amen.*** *The 1662 Book of Common Prayer*

Blessing

Receive God's transforming grace through His Word.

> The Lord Jesus said, "Sanctify them in the truth; your word is truth. As you sent me into the world, so I have sent them into the world. And for their sake I consecrate myself, that they also may be sanctified in truth." *John 17:17-19*

DAY 24
TUESDAY

MORNING PRAYER

Call to Prayer

Hear God call you to abide with Him through His Word.

> In you, O LORD, do I take refuge;
>   let me never be put to shame!
> In your righteousness deliver me and rescue me;
>   incline your ear to me, and save me!
> Be to me a rock of refuge,
>   to which I may continually come;
> you have given the command to save me,
>   for you are my rock and my fortress.   *Psalm 71:1-3*

Adoration

Delight in the goodness of God.

> Praise the LORD!
> **Praise the LORD, O my soul!**
> I will praise the LORD as long as I live;
>   **I will sing praises to my God while I have my being.**   *Psalm 146:1-2*

Confession

Confess your sins to God.

> **Cleanse me from my secret faults, O Lord, and forgive those offenses to Your servant which he has caused in others. I contend not in judgment with You, who are truth; I fear to deceive myself, lest my sin should make me think that I am not sinful. Therefore, I contend not in judgment with You; for if You, Lord, should mark iniquities, O Lord, who shall abide? Amen.** *Augustine*

Thanksgiving

Give thanks to God for His grace and daily mercies.

Psalm

Pray with the people of God in the Psalms.
Psalms 116-118

Scripture Reading

Prayerfully read a portion of God's Word.
Luke 1:39-56

Silence

Keep a moment of quiet stillness to listen to God.

> Fix our hearts on thee, O God, in pure devotion, that the vain pursuits of this world may have no hold upon us, and that we may be changed, by the consuming fire of thy Spirit, into the image and likeness of thy Son, Jesus Christ our Lord, to whom, with thee and the same Spirit, be an honor and glory, world without end. **Amen.**

The Lord's Prayer

Pray the words that the Lord Jesus taught His disciples to pray.

Supplication

Earnestly ask God to accomplish His gracious will.

Almighty and everlasting God whose will it is to restore all things in thy well-beloved Son, the King of kings and the Lord of lords: Mercifully grant that all the peoples of the earth, though now divided and in bondage to sin, may be made free and brought together under His most gracious rule, who liveth and reigneth with thee and the Holy Ghost, one God, now and for ever. **Amen.**

Blessing

Receive God's transforming grace through His Word.

The Lord Jesus said, "I do not ask for these only, but also for those who will believe in me through their word, that they may all be one, just as you, Father, are in me, and I in you, that they also may be in us, so that the world may believe that you have sent me." *John 17:20-21*

EVENING PRAYER

Call to Prayer

Hear God call you to abide with Him through His Word.

Our help is in the name of the LORD,
who made heaven and earth.   *Psalm 124:8*

Adoration

Delight in the goodness of God.

Blessed is he whose help is the God of Jacob,
whose hope is in the LORD his God,
who made heaven and earth,
the sea, and all that is in them,
who keeps faith forever;
who executes justice for the oppressed,
who gives food to the hungry.   *Psalm 146:5-6*

Confession

Confess your sins to God.

Thanksgiving

Give thanks to God for His grace and daily mercies.

Psalm

Pray with the people of God in the Psalms.
Psalm 119:1-32

Scripture Reading

Prayerfully read a portion of God's Word.

Luke 1:39-56

Silence

Keep a moment of quiet stillness to listen to God.

> Behold, I am the servant of the Lord; let it be to me according to your word. **Amen.** *Luke 1:38*

The Lord's Prayer

Pray the words that the Lord Jesus taught His disciples to pray.

Supplication

Earnestly ask God to accomplish His gracious will.

> But you, O LORD, are a shield about me,
>   my glory, and the lifter of my head.
> I cried aloud to the LORD,
>   and he answered me from his holy hill. *Psalm 3:3-4*

Blessing

Receive God's transforming grace through His Word.

> The Lord Jesus said, "I made known to them your name, and I will continue to make it known, that the love with which you have loved me may be in them, and I in them." *John 17:26*

DAY 25

WEDNESDAY

MORNING PRAYER

Call to Prayer

Hear God call you to abide with Him through His Word.

> As a deer pants for flowing streams,
>> so pants my soul for you, O God.
> **My soul thirsts for God,**
>> **for the living God.**
> When shall I come and appear before God?   *Psalm 42:1-2*

Adoration

Delight in the goodness of God.

> *The LORD is my light and my salvation;*
>> *whom shall I fear?*
> **The LORD is the stronghold of my life;**
>> **of whom shall I be afraid?**   *Psalm 27:1*

Confession

Confess your sins to God.

> **O Lord my God, light of the blind, and strength of the weak; yes, also**
> **light of those that see, and strength of the strong—hearken unto my**

soul, and hear it crying out of the depths. Woe is me! . . . Lord, help us to turn and seek You; for not as we have forsaken our Creator have You forsaken Your creation. Let us turn and seek You, for we know You are here in our heart, when we confess to You, when we cast ourselves upon You, and weep in Your bosom, after all our rugged ways; and You gently wipe away our tears, and we weep the more for joy; because You, Lord—not man of flesh and blood—but You, Lord, who made us, remake and comfort us. Amen.   *Augustine*

Thanksgiving
Give thanks to God for His grace and daily mercies.

Psalm
Pray with the people of God in the Psalms.
Psalm 119:33-72

Scripture Reading
Prayerfully read a portion of God's Word.
Galatians 4:4-7

Silence
Keep a moment of quiet stillness to listen to God.

> O God of peace, who hast taught us that in returning and rest we shall be saved, in quietness and in confidence shall be our strength: By the might of thy Spirit lift us, we pray thee, to thy presence, where we may be still and know that thou art God, through Jesus Christ our Lord. **Amen.**
> *To Be a Christian: An Anglican Catechism*

The Lord's Prayer

Pray the words that the Lord Jesus taught His disciples to pray.

Supplication

Earnestly ask God to accomplish His gracious will.

Almighty God, who art afflicted in the afflictions of thy people: Regard with thy tender compassion those in anxiety and distress, bear their sorrows and their cares, supply all their manifold needs, and help both them and us to put our whole trust and confidence in thee, through Jesus Christ our Lord. ***Amen.***

Blessing

Receive God's transforming grace through His Word.

Why are you cast down, O my soul,
    and why are you in turmoil within me?
Hope in God; for I shall again praise him,
    my salvation and my God.   *Psalm 42:11*

EVENING PRAYER

Call to Prayer

Hear God call you to abide with Him through His Word.

> *Deep calls to deep*
> *at the roar of your waterfalls;*
> *all your breakers and your waves*
> *have gone over me.*
> **By day the LORD commands his steadfast love,**
> **and at night his song is with me,**
> **a prayer to the God of my life.** Psalm 42:7-8

Adoration

Delight in the goodness of God.

> Send out your light and your truth;
> let them lead me;
> *let them bring me to your holy hill*
> *and to your dwelling!*
> Then I will go to the altar of God,
> to God my exceeding joy,
> *and I will praise you with the lyre,*
> *O God, my God.* Psalm 43:3-4

Confession

Confess your sins to God.

Thanksgiving

Give thanks to God for His grace and daily mercies.

Psalm

Pray with the people of God in the Psalms.

Psalm 119:73-104

Scripture Reading

Prayerfully read a portion of God's Word.

Galatians 4:4-7

Silence

Keep a moment of quiet stillness to listen to God.

Speak, LORD, for your servant hears. ***Amen***. *1 Samuel 3:9*

The Lord's Prayer

Pray the words that the Lord Jesus taught His disciples to pray.

Supplication

Earnestly ask God to accomplish His gracious will.

As a reconciled Father, take me to be your child; and give me your renewing Spirit, to be in me a principle of holy life, and light, and love, and your seal and witness that I am yours. Let him quicken my dead and hardened heart. Let him enlighten my dark and unbelieving mind, by clearer knowledge and firm belief. Let him turn my will to the ready obedience of your holy will. Let him reveal to my soul the wonders of your love in Christ, and fill it with love to you and my Redeemer, and to all your holy Word and works. ***Amen***.   *Richard Baxter*

Blessing

Receive God's transforming grace through His Word.

In peace I will both lie down and sleep;
    for you alone, O LORD, make me dwell in safety.   *Psalm 4:8*

DAY 26
THURSDAY

MORNING PRAYER

Call to Prayer

Hear God call you to abide with Him through His Word.

Now as they went on their way, Jesus entered a village. And a woman named Martha welcomed him into her house. **And she had a sister called Mary, who sat at the Lord's feet and listened to his teaching.** . . . But the Lord answered her, "Martha, Martha, you are anxious and troubled about many things, but one thing is necessary. **Mary has chosen the good portion, which will not be taken away from her."**

Luke 10:38-39, 41-42

Adoration

Delight in the goodness of God.

The LORD is my shepherd; I shall not want.
> **He makes me lie down in green pastures.**
He leads me beside still waters.
> **He restores my soul.**
He leads me in paths of righteousness
> **for his name's sake.**   *Psalm 23:1-3*

Confession

Confess your sins to God.

> *O You plenteous source of every good and perfect gift, shed abroad the cheering light of Your sevenfold grace over our hearts. Yes, Spirit of love and gentleness, we most humbly implore Your assistance. You know our faults, our failings, our necessities, the dullness of our understanding, the waywardness of our affections, the perverseness of our will. When, therefore, we neglect to practice what we know, visit us, we ask You, with Your grace; enlighten our minds, rectify our desires, correct our wanderings, and pardon our omissions, so that by Your guidance we may be preserved from making shipwreck of faith, and keep a good conscience, and may at length be landed safe in the haven of eternal rest; through Jesus Christ our Lord. Amen.*   Anselm

Thanksgiving

Give thanks to God for His grace and daily mercies.

Psalm

Pray with the people of God in the Psalms.
Psalm 119:105-144

Scripture Reading

Prayerfully read a portion of God's Word.
Philippians 2:5-11

Silence

Keep a moment of quiet stillness to listen to God.

Take our minds, and think through them. Take our lips, and speak through them. Take our hearts, and set them on fire with love for thee.

What we know not, teach us. What we have not, give us. What we are not, make us. For Jesus Christ's sake. ***Amen.***

The Lord's Prayer

Pray the words that the Lord Jesus taught His disciples to pray.

Supplication

Earnestly ask God to accomplish His gracious will.

Look, we beseech thee, with compassion upon those who are now in sorrow and affliction. Comfort them, O Lord, with thy gracious consolations; make them to know that all things work together for good to those who love thee; and grant them a sure trust and confidence in thy fatherly care, through the same Jesus Christ our Lord. ***Amen.***

Blessing

Receive God's transforming grace through His Word.

Jesus himself stood among them, and said to them, "Peace to you!"

Luke 24:36

EVENING PRAYER

Call to Prayer

Hear God call you to abide with Him through His Word.

> Jesus said to her, "I am the resurrection and the life. ***Whoever believes in me, though he die, yet shall he live,*** and everyone who lives and believes in me shall never die. ***Do you believe this?"*** *John 11:25-26*

Adoration

Delight in the goodness of God.

> *She said to him, "Yes, Lord; **I believe that you are the Christ, the Son of God, who is coming into the world."*** *John 11:27*

Confession

Confess your sins to God.

Thanksgiving

Give thanks to God for His grace and daily mercies.

Psalm

Pray with the people of God in the Psalms.
Psalm 119:145-176

Scripture Reading

Prayerfully read a portion of God's Word.
Philippians 2:5-11

Silence

Keep a moment of quiet stillness to listen to God.

> For God alone my soul waits in silence;
>   from him comes my salvation.
> He only is my rock and my salvation,
>   my fortress; I shall not be greatly moved. ***Amen.***   *Psalm 62:1-2*

The Lord's Prayer

Pray the words that the Lord Jesus taught His disciples to pray.

Supplication

Earnestly ask God to accomplish His gracious will.

> Keep watch, dear Lord, with those who work, or watch, or weep this night, and give thine angels charge over those who sleep. Tend the sick, Lord Christ, give rest to the weary, bless the dying, soothe the suffering, pity the afflicted, shield the joyous, and all for thy love's sake. ***Amen.***

Blessing

Receive God's transforming grace through His Word.

> For I am sure that neither death nor life, nor angels nor rulers, nor things present nor things to come, nor powers, nor height nor depth, nor anything else in all creation, will be able to separate us from the love of God in Christ Jesus our Lord.   *Romans 8:38-39*

DAY 27

FRIDAY

MORNING PRAYER

Call to Prayer

Hear God call you to abide with Him through His Word.

> Therefore let everyone who is godly
>   offer prayer to you at a time when you may be found;
> **surely in the rush of great waters,**
>   **they shall not reach him.**
> You are a hiding place for me;
>   *you preserve me from trouble;*
>   *you surround me with shouts of deliverance.*   Psalm 32:6-7

Adoration

Delight in the goodness of God.

> Ascribe to the LORD, O heavenly beings,
>   **ascribe to the LORD glory and strength.**
> Ascribe to the LORD the glory due his name;
>   **worship the LORD in the splendor of holiness.**   Psalm 29:1-2

Confession

Confess your sins to God.

Lord Jesus Christ, great was Your goodness in undertaking my redemption, in consenting to be made sin for me, in conquering all my foes. Great was Your love in manifesting Yourself alive, in showing Your sacred wounds, that every fear might vanish, and every doubt be removed. Great was Your mercy in ascending to heaven, in being crowned and enthroned there to intercede for me, there to help me in temptation, there to open the eternal book, there to receive me finally to Yourself. Great was Your wisdom in devising this means of salvation; bathe my soul in rich consolations of Your resurrection life. O God, pardon all my sins, known and unknown, felt and unfelt, confessed and not confessed, remembered or forgotten. Grant me more and more of the resurrection life: may it rule me, may I walk in its power, and be strengthened through its influence. Amen.

The Valley of Vision: A Collection of Puritan Prayers & Devotions

Thanksgiving

Give thanks to God for His grace and daily mercies.

Psalm

Pray with the people of God in the Psalms.

Psalms 120-125

Scripture Reading

Prayerfully read a portion of God's Word.

John 1:1-18 and Revelation 21:1-8

Silence

Keep a moment of quiet stillness to listen to God.

Fix our hearts on thee, O God, in pure devotion, that the vain pursuits of this world may have no hold upon us, and that we may be changed, by the consuming fire of thy Spirit, into the image and likeness of thy Son, Jesus Christ our Lord, to whom, with thee and the same Spirit, be an honor and glory, world without end. *Amen.*

The Lord's Prayer

Pray the words that the Lord Jesus taught His disciples to pray.

Supplication

Earnestly ask God to accomplish His gracious will.

I pray, Lord Christ, who died for me, that You might have Your own way with me. My Elder Brother, my Lord and my God, I give myself yet again, confidently, because You care to have me and because my very breath is Yours. I will be what You want, You who know all about it and have done everything that I might be Your own—a living glory of gladness. *Amen.*

Adapted from George MacDonald

Blessing

Receive God's transforming grace through His Word.

Many are the sorrows of the wicked,
   but steadfast love surrounds the one who trusts in the LORD.
Be glad in the LORD, and rejoice, O righteous,
   and shout for joy, all you upright in heart!   *Psalm 32:10-11*

EVENING PRAYER

Call to Prayer

Hear God call you to abide with Him through His Word.

> Our soul waits for the LORD;
>> he is our help and our shield.
> **For our heart is glad in him,**
>> **because we trust in his holy name.**
> Let your steadfast love, O LORD, be upon us,
>> even as we hope in you.   *Psalm 33:20-22*

Adoration

Delight in the goodness of God.

> You have turned for me my mourning into dancing;
>> *you have loosed my sackcloth*
>> *and clothed me with gladness,*
> that my glory may sing your praise and not be silent.
>> **O LORD my God, I will give thanks to you forever!**   *Psalm 30:10-12*

Confession

Confess your sins to God.

Thanksgiving

Give thanks to God for His grace and daily mercies.

Psalm

Pray with the people of God in the Psalms.

Psalms 126-131

Scripture Reading

Prayerfully read a portion of God's Word.

John 1:1-18 and Revelation 21:1-8

Silence

Keep a moment of quiet stillness to listen to God.

> Behold, I am the servant of the Lord; let it be to me according to your word. *Amen. Luke 1:38*

The Lord's Prayer

Pray the words that the Lord Jesus taught His disciples to pray.

Supplication

Earnestly ask God to accomplish His gracious will.

> O Merciful Lord God, heavenly Father, whether we sleep or wake, live or die, we are always thine. Wherefore I beseech thee heartily to take care and charge of me, not suffering me to perish in the works of darkness, but kindling the light of thy countenance in my heart, that thy godly knowledge may daily increase in me, through a right and pure faith, and that I may always be found to walk and live after thy wisdom and pleasure, through Jesus Christ our Lord and Savior. *Amen.*

Blessing

Receive God's transforming grace through His Word.

> The God of peace will soon crush Satan under your feet. The grace of our Lord Jesus Christ be with you.   *Romans 16:20*

DAY 28

CHRISTMAS EVE

MORNING PRAYER

Call to Prayer

Hear God call you to abide with Him through His Word.

"I am the LORD; I have called you in righteousness;
   I will take you by the hand and keep you;
I will give you as a covenant for the people,
   a light for the nations,
      to open the eyes that are blind,
   to bring out the prisoners from the dungeon,
      from the prison those who sit in darkness.
I am the LORD; that is my name;
   my glory I give to no other,
      nor my praise to carved idols.   *Isaiah 42:6-8*

Adoration

Delight in the goodness of God.

O LORD, you have searched me and known me!
You know when I sit down and when I rise up;
   you discern my thoughts from afar.
You search out my path and my lying down

and are acquainted with all my ways.
Even before a word is on my tongue,
behold, O LORD, you know it altogether.
You hem me in, behind and before,
and lay your hand upon me.
Such knowledge is too wonderful for me;
it is high; I cannot attain it.   Psalm 139:1-6

Confession

Confess your sins to God.

Almighty and everlasting God, You hate nothing You have made, and You forgive the sins of all who are penitent: Create and make in us new and contrite hearts, that we, worthily lamenting our sins and acknowledging wretchedness, may obtain of You, the God of all mercy, perfect remission and forgiveness; through Jesus Christ our Lord; who lives and reigns with You and the Holy Spirit, one God, for ever and ever. Amen.   To Be a Christian: An Anglican Catechism

Thanksgiving

Give thanks to God for His grace and daily mercies.

Psalm

Pray with the people of God in the Psalms.
Psalms 132-135

Scripture Reading

Prayerfully read a portion of God's Word.
Luke 2:1-21 and Matthew 1:18-25

Silence

Keep a moment of quiet stillness to listen to God.

O God of peace, who hast taught us that in returning and rest we shall be saved, in quietness and in confidence shall be our strength: By the might of thy Spirit lift us, we pray thee, to thy presence, where we may be still and know that thou art God, through Jesus Christ our Lord. ***Amen.***

To Be a Christian: An Anglican Catechism

The Lord's Prayer

Pray the words that the Lord Jesus taught His disciples to pray.

Supplication

Earnestly ask God to accomplish His gracious will.

O Lord, who hast brought us through the darkness of night to the light of morning, and who by thy Holy Spirit dost illumine the darkness of ignorance and sin: We beseech thee of thy loving-kindness to pour thy holy light into our souls, that we may be ever devoted to thee, by whose wisdom we were created, by whose mercy we were redeemed, and by whose providence we are governed, to the honor and glory of thy great name. ***Amen.***

Blessing

Receive God's transforming grace through His Word.

The LORD bless you and keep you;
the LORD make his face to shine upon you and be gracious to you;
the LORD lift up his countenance upon you and give you peace.
Numbers 6:24-26

EVENING PRAYER

Call to Prayer

Hear God call you to abide with Him through His Word.

Trust in the LORD, and do good;
dwell in the land and befriend faithfulness.
Delight yourself in the LORD,
and he will give you the desires of your heart.
Commit your way to the LORD;
trust in him, and he will act.
He will bring forth your righteousness as the light,
and your justice as the noonday.   *Psalm 37:3-6*

Adoration

Delight in the goodness of God.

Where shall I go from your Spirit?
Or where shall I flee from your presence?
If I ascend to heaven, you are there!
If I make my bed in Sheol, you are there!
If I take the wings of the morning
and dwell in the uttermost parts of the sea,
even there your hand shall lead me,
and your right hand shall hold me.
If I say, "Surely the darkness shall cover me,
and the light about me be night,"
even the darkness is not dark to you;
the night is bright as the day,
for darkness is as light with you.   *Psalm 139:7-12*

Confession

Confess your sins to God.

Thanksgiving

Give thanks to God for His grace and daily mercies.

Psalm

Pray with the people of God in the Psalms.

Psalms 136-138

Scripture Reading

Prayerfully read a portion of God's Word.

Luke 2:1-21 and Matthew 1:18-25

Silence

Keep a moment of quiet stillness to listen to God.

> Speak, LORD, for your servant hears. ***Amen.*** *1 Samuel 3:9*

The Lord's Prayer

Pray the words that the Lord Jesus taught His disciples to pray.

Supplication

Earnestly ask God to accomplish His gracious will.

> Almighty God, who hast given us thy only-begotten Son to take our nature upon him, and as at this time to be born of a pure virgin: Grant that we, being regenerate and made thy children by adoption and grace, may daily be renewed by thy Holy Spirit, through the same our Lord Jesus Christ, who liveth and reigneth with thee and the same Spirit, ever one God, world without end. ***Amen.*** *The 1662 Book of Common Prayer*

Blessing

Receive God's transforming grace through His Word.

"Death is swallowed up in victory."

"O death, where is your victory?

O death, where is your sting?"

The sting of death is sin, and the power of sin is the law. But thanks be to God, who gives us the victory through our Lord Jesus Christ.

1 Corinthians 15:55-57

Appendix

∿

Praying the Psalms

Day 1
Morning Prayer: Psalms 1-5
Evening Prayer: Psalms 6-8

Day 2
Morning Prayer: Psalms 9-11
Evening Prayer: Psalms 12-14

Day 3
Morning Prayer: Psalms 15-17
Evening Prayer: Psalm 18

Day 4
Morning Prayer: Psalms 19-21
Evening Prayer: Psalms 22-23

Day 5
Morning Prayer: Psalms 24-26
Evening Prayer: Psalms 27-29

Day 6
Morning Prayer: Psalms 30-31
Evening Prayer: Psalms 32-34

Day 7
Morning Prayer: Psalms 35-36
Evening Prayer: Psalm 37

Day 8
Morning Prayer: Psalms 38-40
Evening Prayer: Psalms 41-43

Day 9
Morning Prayer: Psalms 44-46
Evening Prayer: Psalms 47-49

Day 10
Morning Prayer: Psalms 50-52
Evening Prayer: Psalms 53-55

Day 11
Morning Prayer: Psalms 56-58
Evening Prayer: Psalms 59-61

Day 12
Morning Prayer: Psalms 62-64
Evening Prayer: Psalms 65-67

Day 13
Morning Prayer: Psalm 68
Evening Prayer: Psalms 69-70

Day 14
Morning Prayer: Psalms 71-72
Evening Prayer: Psalms 73-74

Day 15
Morning Prayer: Psalms 75-77
Evening Prayer: Psalm 78

Day 16
Morning Prayer: Psalms 79-81
Evening Prayer: Psalms 82-85

Day 17
Morning Prayer: Psalms 86-88
Evening Prayer: Psalm 89

Day 18
Morning Prayer: Psalms 90-92
Evening Prayer: Psalms 93-94

Day 19
Morning Prayer: Psalms 95-97
Evening Prayer: Psalms 98-101

Day 20
Morning Prayer: Psalms 102-103
Evening Prayer: Psalm 104

Day 21
Morning Prayer: Psalm 105
Evening Prayer: Psalm 106

Day 22
Morning Prayer: Psalm 107
Evening Prayer: Psalms 108-109

Day 23
Morning Prayer: Psalms 110-113
Evening Prayer: Psalms 114-115

Day 24
Morning Prayer: Psalms 116-118
Evening Prayer: Psalm 119:1-32

Day 25
Morning Prayer: Psalm 119:33-72
Evening Prayer: Psalm 119:73-104

Day 26
Morning Prayer: Psalm 119:105-144
Evening Prayer: Psalm 119:145-176

Day 27
Morning Prayer: Psalms 120-125
Evening Prayer: Psalms 126-131

Day 28
Morning Prayer: Psalms 132-135
Evening Prayer: Psalms 136-138

Day 29
Morning Prayer: Psalms 139-141
Evening Prayer: Psalms 142-143

Day 30
Morning Prayer: Psalms 144-146
Evening Prayer: Psalms 147-150

Reading the Storyline of the Bible

Day 1 | *The First Sunday in Advent*
Isaiah 60:1-3

Day 2
Genesis 1:1-2:3

Day 3
Psalm 8 and Genesis 2:4-25

Day 4
Genesis 3 and 4

Day 5
Genesis 6 and 9

Day 6
Genesis 12; 18:1-15; 22

Day 7
Genesis 28:10-22 and 45:1-28

Day 8 | *The Second Sunday in Advent*
Isaiah 9:2-7 and Isaiah 11:1-9

Day 9
Exodus 3 and 15:1-21

Day 10
Exodus 19 and 20

Day 11
Exodus 40

Day 12
Joshua 1 and 24:1-28

Day 13
Judges 2:11-23 and 1 Samuel 4:1-11

Day 14
1 Samuel 8 and 17

Day 15 | *The Third Sunday in Advent*
Micah 5:2-5

Day 16
2 Samuel 7 and Psalm 51

Day 17
1 Kings 3 and 8:1-21

Day 18
1 Kings 18:16-40 and 2 Kings 17:1-18

Day 19
2 Kings 24-25 and Jeremiah 7:1-15

Day 20
Psalm 137:1-6 and Haggai 1

Day 21
Isaiah 40

Day 22 | *The Fourth Sunday in Advent*
Malachi 4 and Luke 1:5-25, 57-80

Excerpts from the Westminster Larger Catechism on Prayer

Question 178: What is prayer?

Answer: Prayer is an offering up of our desires unto God, in the name of Christ, by the help of his Spirit; with confession of our sins, and thankful acknowledgment of his mercies.

Question 180: What is it to pray in the name of Christ?

Answer: To pray in the name of Christ is, in obedience to his command, and in confidence on his promises, to ask mercy for his sake; not by bare mentioning of his name, but by drawing our encouragement to pray, and our boldness, strength, and hope of acceptance in prayer, from Christ and his mediation.

Question 181: What are we to pray in the name of Christ?

Answer: The sinfulness of man, and his distance from God by reason thereof, being so great, as that we can have no access into his presence without a mediator; and there being none in heaven or earth appointed to, or fit for, that glorious work but Christ alone, we are to pray in no other name but his only.

Question 182: How doth the Spirit help us to pray?

Answer: We not knowing what to pray for as we ought, the Spirit helpeth our infirmities, by enabling us to understand both for whom, and what, and how prayer is to be made; and by working and quickening in our hearts (although not in all persons, nor at all times, in the same measure) those apprehensions, affections, and graces which are requisite for the right performance of that duty.

Question 185: How are we to pray?

Answer: We are to pray with an awful apprehension of the majesty of God, and deep sense of our own unworthiness, necessities, and sins; with penitent, thankful, and enlarged hearts; with understanding, faith, sincerity, fervency, love, and perseverance, waiting upon him, with humble submission to his will.

Question 186: What rule hath God given for our direction in the duty of prayer?

Answer: The whole Word of God is of use to direct us in the duty of prayer, but the special rule of direction is that form of prayer which our Savior Christ taught his disciples, commonly called the Lord's Prayer.

Question 187: How is the Lord's Prayer to be used?

Answer: The Lord's Prayer is not only for direction, as a pattern, according to which we are to make other prayers; but may also be used as a prayer, so that it be done with understanding, faith, reverence, and other graces necessary to the right performance of the duty of prayer.

The Lord's Prayer

Traditional

Our Father, who art in heaven,
hallowed be thy name;
thy kingdom come;
thy will be done;
on earth as it is in heaven.
Give us this day our daily bread.
And forgive us our trespasses,
as we forgive those who trespass against us.
And lead us not into temptation;
but deliver us from evil.
For thine is the kingdom,
the power and the glory,
for ever and ever.
Amen.

Contemporary

Our Father in heaven,
hallowed be your name;
your kingdom come;
your will be done, on earth as it is in heaven.
Give us this day our daily bread.
And forgive us our debts, as we forgive our debtors.
And lead us not into temptation but deliver us from evil.
For yours is the kingdom, and the power,
And the glory, forever. Amen.

The Apostle's Creed

*The Apostle's Creed is an early declaration of the Christian
faith, summing up essentials of right belief.*

Traditional

I believe in God, the Father almighty,

maker of heaven and earth;

And in Jesus Christ, his only Son, our Lord;

who was conceived by the Holy Ghost,

born of the Virgin Mary,

suffered under Pontius Pilate,

was crucified, dead, and buried.

He descended into hell.

The third day he rose again from the dead.

He ascended into heaven,

and sitteth on the right hand of God the Father almighty.

From thence he shall come to judge the quick and the dead.

I believe in the Holy Ghost,

the holy catholic Church*,

the communion of saints,

the forgiveness of sins,

the resurrection of the body,

and the life everlasting. Amen.

Contemporary

I believe in God, the Father almighty,

creator of heaven and earth.

I believe in Jesus Christ, his only Son, our Lord.

He was conceived by the power of the Holy Spirit

and born of the Virgin Mary.

He suffered under Pontius Pilate,

was crucified, died, and was buried.

He descended to the dead.

On the third day he rose again.

He ascended into heaven,

and is seated at the right hand of the Father.

He will come again to judge the living and the dead.

I believe in the Holy Spirit,

the holy catholic Church*,

the communion of saints,

the forgiveness of sins,

the resurrection of the body,

and the life everlasting. Amen.

*meaning the universal Christian church—all believers in Jesus Christ

The Nicene Creed

*The Nicene Creed is a more detailed declaration of faith
adopted at the Council of Nicaea in AD 325 that has served as a
faithful summary of right belief for the whole Church.*

We believe in one God,
the Father, the Almighty,
maker of heaven and earth,
of all that is,
seen and unseen.

We believe in one Lord, Jesus Christ,
the only Son of God,
eternally begotten of the Father,
God from God, Light from Light,
true God from true God,
begotten, not made,
of one Being with the Father;
through him all things were made.
For us and for our salvation he came down from heaven,
was incarnate from the Holy Spirit and the Virgin Mary
and was made man.
For our sake he was crucified under Pontius Pilate;
he suffered death and was buried.
On the third day he rose again
in accordance with the Scriptures;
he ascended into heaven
and is seated at the right hand of the Father.

He will come again in glory to judge the living and the dead,
and his kingdom will have no end.

We believe in the Holy Spirit,
the Lord, the giver of life,
who proceeds from the Father and the Son,
who with the Father and the Son is worshipped and glorified,
who has spoken through the prophets.
We believe in one holy catholic and apostolic Church.
We acknowledge one baptism for the forgiveness of sins.
We look for the resurrection of the dead,
and the life of the world to come.
Amen.

NOTES

Prayers taken from The Anglican Church in North America, *To Be a Christian: An Anglican Catechism* (Wheaton: Crossway, 2020).

Augustine, Ambrose, Anselm, John Calvin, and Richard Baxter prayers taken from Jonathan Gibson, *Be Thou My Vision: A Liturgy for Daily Worship* (Wheaton: Crossway, 2021).

George MacDonald prayer adapted from The Northumbria Community Trust Ltd., *Celtic Daily Prayer: Prayers and Readings from the Northumbria Community* (New York: HarperCollins, 2002).

Praying the Psalms is taken from The Book of Common Prayer.

Reading the Story-Line of the Bible is adapted from Paige Vanosky and Craig Bartholomew, *The 30-Minute Bible: God's Story for Everyone* (Downers Grove: InterVarsity Press, 2021).

Westminster Larger Catechism excerpts taken from *The Westminster Confession of Faith and Catechisms as adopted by the Presbyterian Church in America.*

Unless otherwise indicated, written prayers taken from The 1662 Book of Common Prayer: International Edition *(IVP Academic 2021). All rights to new material and updated language reserved.*

PARK CITIES PRESBYTERIAN CHURCH

4124 Oak Lawn Ave., Dallas, TX 75219

pcpc.org